# Mysterious Powell Lake

A Collection of Historical Tales
by Carla Mobley

hancock

house

*To Lois
With Love from Bud.
JUNE 1987*

**ISBN** 0-88839-983-9

Copyright© Carla Mobley 1984

Printed in Canada by Friesen Printers

Published simultaneously in Canada and the United States by

**HANCOCK HOUSE PUBLISHERS LTD.**
19313 Zero Ave., Surrey, B.C.  V3S 5J9

**HANCOCK HOUSE PUBLISHERS INC.**
1431 Harrison Avenue, Blaine, WA  98230

# Contents

Acknowledgements .................................................................... 4
Introduction ............................................................................. 5
Map ......................................................................................... 6
Time Line ................................................................................ 8
Poems ................................................................................... 10
Legends of Powell Lake ....................................................... 11
Memories .............................................................................. 14
Cassiar .................................................................................. 23
Powell Lake Monster .......................................................... 23
Olsen Valley ......................................................................... 25
Tom Ogburn ........................................................................ 35
Powell Lake Farm ............................................................... 37
A Prospector's Memories .................................................... 41
Nick Hudema ....................................................................... 44
Powell Lake Shingle Mill .................................................... 49
Doc Jameson ........................................................................ 53
The Toklat ............................................................................ 56
The Laundry ......................................................................... 57
Emile Gordon ....................................................................... 59
The Japanese Internment .................................................... 60
Fires at the Shingle Mill ..................................................... 64
Ray Sims .............................................................................. 65
The Andersons ..................................................................... 67
P.R. Lockie ........................................................................... 71
The Snow Survey ................................................................. 76
Jack Wilson .......................................................................... 80
Billy-Goat Smith .................................................................. 82
Powell Lake Today .............................................................. 91
References ............................................................................. 94
Index ..................................................................................... 95

4

# Acknowledgements

4

I would like to thank all my friends who encouraged and helped me, especially those who so willingly shared memories with me: Golden Stanley, Evan Sadler, Roger Simard, Mr. and Mrs. Oren Olson, Bill Merrit, Gordie Dycks, Mrs. Michael Savage, Mr. and Mrs. Stewart Lambert, Chuck Wilcocks, Tony Mathews, Bertram Wilson, Curly Woodward, Harold and Sid Allman, Jackie Timothy, Graeme McCahon, Gladys Cockril, Alice Cluff, Mr. and Mrs. Roger Taylor and Henry Pavid.

I am also indebted to Penny Copley, Laura Everett, Doreen Herie, Jim Southern, Peter and Margaret Behr, Robert Foster, Penny Kanigan, Terry Davis, Bob Dice, Dianne Louke, Mary Mobley, Ethel Ross, Donna Summerfelt, Ron Tellier and Eileen Pense. All are friends who encouraged and helped me whenever I needed someone to do just that.

I am particularly grateful for the partnership I shared with Karen Southern who is a fellow writer, Ann Winberg and Brenda Falconer for their dedicated typing and office help, and to Ann Trousdall and Juliet Potter for their photographic skills. I would also like to acknowledge Doug Mobley who has proof-read and developed pictures.

Thanks also to the New Horizons group and the government for the Winter Works program which allowed me to write. Thanks also to the Powell River News whose information has been invaluable.

Finally I would like to dedicate this book to Mom and Dad and Uncle Jim who taught me always to listen for the loons.

# Introduction

At the risk of sounding sentimental, I will admit that I feel it is no accident that I am here in Powell River writing a local history. One of the first things I discovered in my research was the name of my grandfather, Carl Hult. It was so exciting to talk to Oren Olson and Evan Sadler about Carl and his sister, Mamie. My fascination for the lake which began three years ago continues. In researching I realize that I have hardly scratched the surface of the history. A book could, and should be written about Olsen Valley, The Shingle Mill, the logging history, or any one of the lake characters. People who are concerned with the conservation of history are invited to send material, tapes and letters to The Powell River Museum, P.O. Box 42, Powell River.

During my research for the book I have continually been impressed by the love the old-timers reveal for the land and the people of the area. This environmental enthusiasm was very moving to me. And let me also add here, that I use the word "old-timer" as meaning residents that have been in the area since 1930. It doesn't necessarily mean old.

I must admit I also gained more of an appreciation for the Powell River area. In a world that is over-populated we are certainly fortunate to live near the uninhabited rain forest that is so close at hand. Powell Lake has such a special quality that rouses emotion in all who live nearby, that at times I imagine myself to be a scribe writing of a holy place.

# POWELL LAKE REGION

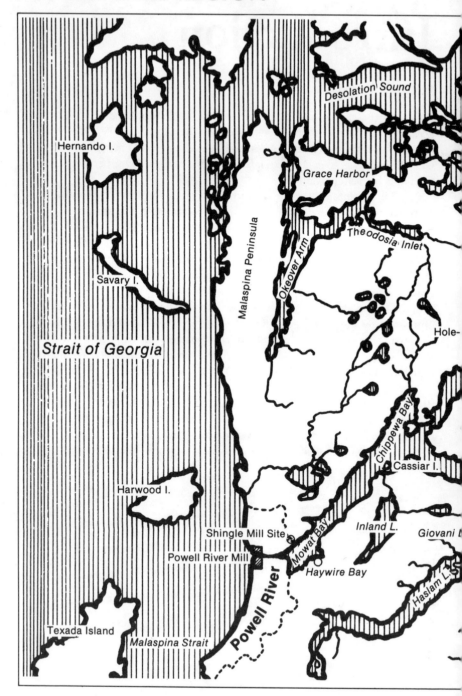

Desolation Sound

Hernando I.

Grace Harbor

Theodosia Inlet

Malaspina Peninsula

Okeover Arm

Savary I.

Hole-

Strait of Georgia

Chippewa Bay

Cassiar I.

Harwood I.

Shingle Mill Site

Mowat Bay

Inland L.

Giovani

Powell River Mill

Haywire Bay

Powell River

Texada Island

Malaspina Strait

Haslam L

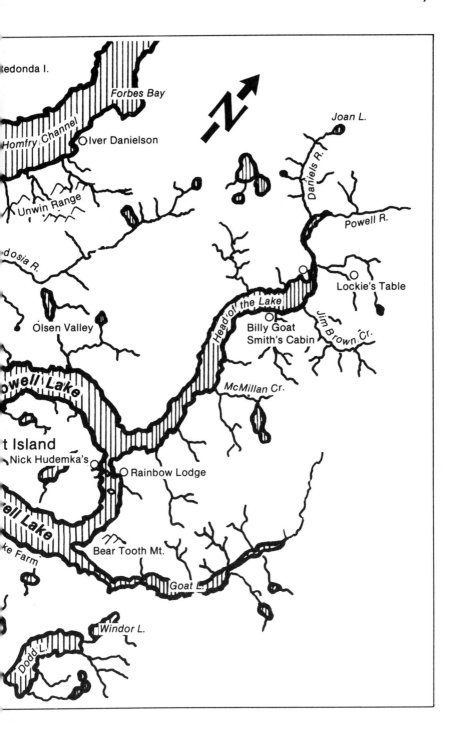

# Time Line

1791 — George Vancouver passes the area

1880 — Townsite named after Dr. Israel Powell

1900 — Logging in Wildwood

1906 — Tom Ogburn arrives in area

— Stanford White murdered in New York

1907 — Japanese enter B.C. fishing industry and mobs attack orientals in Vancouver

1908 — Andy Anderson comes to Powell River

1909 — Dr. Henderson comes to Powell River

1910 — Powell River Company begins construction

— First business set up (China Block)

— Olsen Valley opens for settlement

1911 — Penstocks at mill break

— Jack Wilson comes to Powell River

— Bloedel, Stewart and Welch begin logging at Myrtle point

1912 — Fire at Olsen Valley

— Mill starts operation

1913 — Olsons move to Olsen Valley

— 600 men employed at the mill

1914 — 1918: WWI

1915 — Bridge at Cedar Street built

— F.H. Swift surveys lake

— Last Spike

1917 — First car in Powell River

— Workmen's compensation board created

1918 — First aeroplane lands on Powell Lake

1920 — Olsons leave Olsen Valley

— Powell River Company changes from horses to trucks

1921 — Government operated liquor stores

1924 — Company raises dam

1927 — First pension cheque
1928 — Fire at the laundry at the Shingle Mill
    — First provincial census taken
1929 — Goat Island created as Game Reserve
1930 — Hulks brought to form breakwater
1931 — Fire at Shingle mill
1932 — Anderson's mill started
1933 — Scarlet Fever epidemic
1934 — Bear Tooth mountain climbed by P.R. Lockie and R.H. Simmons
    — Serious unemployment
    — Dr. Henderson dies
1936 — Company leases Rainbow Lodge
1937 — Billy Goat's boat wrecked
1938 — First Snow Survey done by Lockie
1939 — Canada declares war on Germany
1940 — Nick Hudemka comes to Powell Lake
1941 — Early founders of mill, Brooks and Scanlon die same year
1942 — Japanese internment completed
1945 — End of WWII
    — Fire at Shingle mill
1946 — IWA strike
1947 — Gulf Steam runs aground at Dinner Rock
1948 — Diotte Airways Ltd. started
1949 — Japanese allowed back on coast
1950 — Sims plane crashes
1951 — Shingle mill's final fire
1954 — Road-ferry link to Vancouver becomes a reality
1957 — Schiel climbs Bear Tooth
1959 — Marion Smith visits Billy-Goat
1968 — Snow survey done by helicopter
1970 — Powell Lake farm bought by Vonnegut and friends
    — Buildings at Olsen Valley burned
1976 — Andy Anderson's mill equipment sold to Burnaby

# Poems

### Powell Lake I

That hermit
my favourite one
lived there for years
loved the bears
making trails for him
watching him at his work.

But hummingbirds
flitting, buzzing, flying
(You can't even shoot them)
They tried to take his tears
right off his face
tried to sip nectar from
the corner of his left eye

tried to pierce his mind.

by Carla Mobley

## Powell Lake II

Under the shadows of the northern lights — how real can we be
how real can we be — in the still grey mountains
of the silent night when eagles fly over stars
when tears drop fast in the roots of trees
with visions of mountain goats, rainbows
ferns and the sound of a flute.

A forest madness: maybe you have sensed it.

the green of vines you touch the middle of the night
choking when you walk the path or touch only bones
under moss to create a desert, or panic to remember
the beginning sets forth in each seed of
more green.

Look, the path is twisted, circular
through immense foliage of dancing patterns
of thick shadows, lightning
in the moist spring leaves.

by Carla Mobley

# Legends of Powell Lake

## told by Jackie Timothy

A Sliammon village was once situated at the mouth of Powell River. It was called Tesquiot (TEE-squt), and this is where the salmon used to spawn every fall.

Powell Lake was used for travel to the head of Jervis Inlet where there was excellent fishing and hunting. The Indians would take their canoes to the end of Powell Lake and portage the rest of the way. This trail wasn't known to many people.

There's a story of a "Hamitsha," a large bird that would fly the skies. This bird was as large as a human being and had a huge crook on the beak which he used to open a man's head and eat his brains.

There is also a story of a special man with supernatural powers who got his energy and strength through the cedar boughs. He'd get hold of the branches and break them in a certain way. The cedars were the source of his power.

This man was so strong he was able to cross over the mountain ranges to visit the other Indians on the other side. He came back and told the people here that there was life on the other side of the mountain, that there was life beyond the places they could see. But they didn't believe him.

This special man decided to prove that he was right, and he went all the way through the mountains and stole a newborn baby. When he came back the people were amazed that life existed beyond the mountains. The man touched and blessed the people and made trails to Bella Coola and Tlinget.

The Bella Coola were a fierce tribe who liked war. Maybe they were jealous of this man, maybe they believed that if they killed him that they would possess his strength and power. One day a large group of Bella Coola cornered him in a river but since there were too many enemies for him to fight, he dove under the logs. The Bella Coola waited until they thought he had drowned. All of a sudden they heard weird noises coming from the forest. The Bella Coola were so frightened they ran away. After they had gone he came out of the water.

There was a battle at Goat River and one at the top of the lake. The Bella Coola would come from the coast and drive the Sliammon people up the lake.

On one raid the Bella Coola wiped out all the Coast Salish people, except for five. The Bella Coola brought in more warriors wanting to eradicate the whole tribe, but the warriors were destroyed in a rock slide. Later when the Coast Salish went up the lake to pick berries, the families said they could hear the rocks crying because of the people who had died there, they could feel the sadness. This is the story of the weeping rocks.

During the battle at Goat Lake, the Coast Salish were running out of arrows. They stationed themselves at the top of the mountain there, and while they were there they found a soft shiny rock that was easy to shape into arrowheads. It sounds like this rock might have been gold.

Jackie Timothy

# Memories
## by Curly Woodward

*The following information is taken almost directly from an interview with Mr. Wilfred "Curly" Woodward, one of Powell River's earliest citizens.*

The town is called Powell River after the river which is one of the shortest in the world, if not the shortest, and both the lake and the river were named after Dr. Israel Powell who was an Indian agent and a very prominent man in Victoria. He came to this area in the middle 1800s. Dr. Powell was the first grand master of the Masonic Lodge in British Columbia. He had a wonderful career, and he and Judge Begbie's names were linked together because they both fought to preserve B.C. from American influence.

Around 1980 there was some argument about the relative value of water in Powell Lake and in Haslam Lake. People were not aware of the fact that in Powell Lake at depths below four feet there are chemicals in the water, especially methane. Powell Lake water may seem pure but there is a gradual dissipation of methane that is still generating when the water below the four foot mark is disturbed. Methane, a gas, can be used as a fuel, but being in such slow dispersion is only marginally harmful. The unknown factor is how much more methane and other gases are still being generated by bark, leaves, etc. that sink to the bottom of the lake.

The chemicals are in the deep water because it is salt-water which was trapped there nearly 10,000 years ago. It is believed that Powell Lake was once an inlet of the sea and was cut off from the Pacific when the land rose thousands of years ago after the disappearance of glacial ice several thousands of feet thick. When the ice sheet retreated, salt-water was trapped in the Powell Lake basin at a depth of at least two feet above the present sea level. The scientists know the water was this high because the fossil remains of sea organisms have been found on the surrounding mountains at that height.

The maximum length of the lake is 26.8 miles, the maximum width is 4.37 miles, and the deepest part of the lake is 1,174 feet, according to National Research Council figures taken in 1974.

There is a high point in the lake near the Wildwood Bridge that created a natural falls in the old days. Of course the mill never would have come to this location without the falls because it is the source of power.

They brought the water down in penstocks from the canal that they built below the headgates.

It was early 1911 when the penstocks broke. They used wood stave pipes in those days. When I was four years old I remember the repairs they were doing, putting in the new steel penstocks. We could hear the rivetters working all night long because we lived just across the point above number ten machine.

The water from Powell Lake was used in three ways. It was used to turn the water-wheels which were under the grinders that converted the wood to pulp, and it was used for water power for generating electricity. The grinding process has changed and now most water is used in generating electricity. The electrical output of the plant is approximately thirty thousand megawatts of power. The mill consumes almost as much water in a day as the city of New York does. Of course there are many general uses for water in the mill as well, for cleaning the machines and things like that, they use a remarkable amount of water.

In the old days, the people in the townsite used power from the mill for domestic purposes for a nominal sum. They used to heat the houses all

Curly Woodward

winter by turning on their electric stoves and opening the oven doors. It proved an awful shock when the hydro came in. My first hydro bill was around seventy dollars for one month. I got the shock of my life, and was thankful that the first bill was only indicative of what my consumption for the month had been. It would have cost me almost as much as I was being paid at that time.

The Powell River dam as originally built didn't have any spillgates, excess water simply spilled over the crest. The crest was a two-level deal. At the east end close to the locks, the elevation was 260 feet. Over the more westerly section of the dam, it was five feet higher.

In 1924 the dam was raised. The new crest was raised twelve feet and above that there were a series of spill gates allowing the lake to rise to an elevation of 284 feet.

When they raised the lake those twelve feet it changed the bays, the headlands and everything else. I imagine people from 1912, '13 and '14 would have had a hard time recognizing the salient points of the lake. There were so many more bays and headlands in those days. When the lake was raised it left a lake full of stumps sticking out of the water in contrast to the old days when the shores were clear. Throughout the years these stumps have caused numerous accidents. It wasn't all a positive gain except economically. The lake presented a more charming vista prior to the raising of the dam. Some of the wild flowers and other flora native to the shoreline were lost. It certainly flooded back far in the valleys and flooded considerable fertile land, and this gave rise to land claims with people seeking compensation for what they had lost. Many people wanted to live an independent lifestyle on the lake, when it was raised they had to go higher up the slopes. In most cases there was little compensation for land or lost resources, so there were some very hard feelings in the early days resulting in court cases that engendered lasting animosities. Cassiar Island was reduced to one third its size with only the less fertile part remaining.

With the raising of the dam in 1924, the three generators they were using were able to increase the output of power by ten per cent. It was an increase of about one megawatt. One megawatt is one million watts or 1,341 horse power.

A new ten megawatt generator was added and increased the electrical power by a total of eleven megawatts or about fifteen thousand horse power. Later the top of the dam wall and gates was modified to allow a lake level of 285 feet. To this day this is the lake's maximum level.

Later when the water-driven pulp grinders were phased out and a more modern electric generator was installed, the electrical generating capacity was increased by thirty megawatts. The new generator proved much more efficient than the old water wheels, and as a result, more power could be derived from the same amount of water.

I remember the old days at the mouth of the river. Three to four years after the dam had been built the salmon were still coming back to the river, and the Indians in the past obviously must have used this spawning ground as a great food source. We were just kids and we were fascinated by the way the Indian women went down into the water with the water coming down at quite a speed from the dam, and they were out there with tree branches fashioned in the following way. They would cut a main branch about four feet long with a smaller branch attached, that was at a sharp angle to it, almost looking like a fishing hook. They would sharpen the point of the stick at the long end away from the hook-like piece, and thread it through the gills of the large salmon, and by the time they had this filled they must have had several hundred pounds of fish on it. They were careful to keep the load under the water so that it would reduce the weight to a minimum so they could drag it to shore. We were fascinated by it all. You'd often see a salmon that would be almost four feet long.

We would always venture down as kids have always done, and try to get in on the action, but we got chased away in a hurry. In those days there were still stories about savagery so when they told us to leave we took their words seriously and removed our hides to a safe distance away.

When I look back on this lost treasure of salmon, lost through the short-sightedness of man, I believe that this could still be reversed if man's new knowledge of fish ladders could be brought into play and a resource once lost could be re-established for the good of all.

The lake was prospected in the early days and I can remember under the old bridge that used to be at the end of Cedar Street, there were many old York boats, the type used in the fur trade. They were old and rotting away even at that time. So there's an indication that the lake was used for travel; some rumors have it that some of the prospectors who went up to Cassiar went in through the head of the lake.

The lake has been a great source of timber. Brooks-Bidlake had a mill on the west side of the lake northwest of the new bridge, and that was followed by the Jameson Mill which turned out shingles for many years. It used to be quite a sight to see the good old-fashioned hard-tired trucks, two Republics. They loaded the scows down at the government dock for many destinations.

A lot of large timber came out of timber claims around the lake, and there are large reserves still back there, but they are not very readily accessible. If the helicopters or dirigibles could be used to lift the timber out, we will see great activity on Powell Lake once again.

Burning log jam at Powell Lake outlet

By the way, speaking of loggers, we had some wonderful characters around here. Jim Springer was a very famous man, a skilled logger who came here in the 1880s and logged in many local areas.

Two of the colorful personalities that directed the progress of The Powell River Company during their first fifteen years of operation, were Dr. Dwight Brooks and M.J. Scanlon. These men travelled the continent visiting their extensive operations. They maintained a close watch on the logging concessions at Stillwater. Dr. Brooks wore a battered felt hat, and comfortable nondescript clothing, but his partner M.J. Scanlon was a little more "dapper."

The logging railroad used to come down beside the river and down through the townsite below the Patricia Theatre, then along the ocean shore to Michigan Landing which was later named Willingdon Beach after the Governor General Willingdon who once was the Governor General of India. At that beach they used to unload the logs off the dock.

The Union Steamships also stopped at the dock to serve the camp at the beach. These ships were important to the whole development of the coast. I was on dayboats that took as long as fifteen hours to arrive at Vancouver. They'd stop at every little dock and every little cove. They performed a wonderful function by keeping life in these small places that wouldn't have been able to exist or develop . . . the logging camps or anything else. The captains of these ships must have known thousands of people in these little settlements. They were looked upon with much affection.

The government dock was built on a rock-fill that went out from the shore below Marine Avenue by the mill. It had decking on it and dock facilities including a large warehouse. It was phased out in 1940 when Westview dock came into being. We used to go down there quite often. They used to park a lot of fishboats there and we used to climb up on the pile driver and dive off about thirty feet up. Sometimes the pulp used to be deep on the bottom and if a fellow didn't come up in a hurry the other fellows would go down for him and pull him up. He'd be buried up to his waist in stinking pulp. So you can see there were some disadvantages to this industrialization. Eventually they made a beach further down the shore because the pulp was too much in the original location.

Picnic on Powell Lake

Talking about Powell Lake in general in the early days, I think one of the real things that started to distinguish people socially was the kind of boat they had on the lake. Doctor Henderson had a beautiful speed boat and he was Number One, and Number Two was Director Norman Lang's boat. Everyone seemed to have a boat. It was the only place we could escape in those days. We could go twenty-six miles up the lake. There were cabins galore and far more boats on the lake than now.

Picnic on Powell Lake

Most of the cabins were miles up the lake, at the head, in the narrows, and in the Hole-in-the-Wall until around 1916. Then they started locating at One-mile and Three-mile Bays, Henderson Bay, Mowatt Bay and across the lake at Loon Falls. These float cabins were named things like "Newby's Seldom-Inn," and "Bide-A-Wee." There was even a cabin called "King Tut's Tomb."

On the first of July there was a race around Cassiar Island and back, and Doc Henderson usually managed to win it, but he'd lose it sometimes on the lapsed time because they'd have handicaps for horse power. The people would all stand on shore watching the boats go out.

Old Doc would be coming smiling down the lake first, and then he'd find out he came in ninth because of the handicapping and he didn't like that very much. The lake was a real escape for workers and their families especially before cars became available.

Boat house on Powell Lake

A picnic on Scout Mountain overlooking Powell Lake — 1916

Boat house 1916

Preparing for a boat race — July 1, 1914

# Cassiar

Cassiar was a hand-logger that lived on Cassiar Island, in the early 1900s, but when The Powell River Company flooded the lake, the island became smaller and Cassiar said there wasn't enough room. All the fertile land on that island was lost in the flooding.

Cassiar moved to Goat Lake and set up a homestead there. He only had a row boat and every Saturday he would row down to the Post Office to get his mail. "If the mail wasn't sorted, you should have heard the language he came out with," Evan Sadler recalls.

Curly Woodward remembers the one day that Cassiar came to school. "I imagine he thought he was whispering," he says, "but he had a voice like a fog horn and his language was spiced with the choicest words. Our education was certainly expanded that day."

One day Cassiar "went missing." They thought he might have had a heart attack, but his body was never found, only his boat.

That wasn't unusual," Evan explains. "Powell Lake seldom gives up its dead."

# Powell Lake
# Monster

This legend was originally collected and written by Golden Stanley, and printed in Powell River News in April, 1952.

Tolfeba was a reptile that lived under the villages and ate the dead that the Indians buried. He was such a huge monster that he was always hungry. He poisoned the drinking water so he could have more food. When the Indians gathered together for a meeting about the water they decided to starve the monster by burying their dead in trees.

When they did this the monster became enraged. He rocked the villages to frighten everyone and the deer and bears ran away from the area. As a result a famine threatened to destroy the natives. In an effort to survive they moved their villages. For a while that seemed to work but Tolfeba found them again. They moved again. And again. Eventually they went to the area now known as Cranberry Lake, and they set their village at the northern end of a creek which used to drain into Powell Lake. Again the monster found them.

They moved their homes to a low island in the middle of Cranberry Lake hoping that the monster could only survive underground and that he would drown if he tried to go over to the island. Unfortunately Tolfeba was totally at home in the water, and he diseased the whole lake.

The old chief gathered his people together again, and this time they decided to make a strong rope out of cedar bark and rawhide.

By spring they had completed the rope and had also obtained an anchor bolt and ring from some white traders. They fastened the anchor bolt and ring to a huge boulder at the north end of the lake.

As the monster passed by the island the young men managed to slip the rope around the monster and pull the rope tight around his belly. The sea monster leapt up in the water and came down with an enormous splash. The spray from its writhing black body soaked the surrounding hills. At one time it whipped its long serpent tail up against the side of the hill on the west side. It smashed every tree beneath its tail, and as it slid back into the water it dragged all the soil with it.

This strip of bare land can still be seen because nothing but moss and a few scattered shrubs have been able to survive there since that day.

The Indian men struggled with the monster until they had him securely tied at the end of the lake. That night they had a party to celebrate their victory over Tolfeba. The women bandaged the sores and wounds of the men and massaged their aching muscles. Everyone was happy. No longer would they be plagued by a creature who caused death and feasted upon their dead. Finally they would be able to bury their dead without feeding this gluttonous enemy.

As the festivities progressed into the night with singing and dancing around the fire, they gradually became aware that the ground under their feet was becoming soggy. The lake was rising. There was a sense of panic. Only the men could swim and they couldn't desert their families. A few were able to get boats, but most drowned.

The few that escaped stood sadly on the shore. They found that Tolfeba had crawled onto the land, and in an attempt to escape he had pushed up the gravel and sand and dammed the creek. He had escaped to Powell Lake.

Mr. Stanley recalls Chief Toma telling him of this monster in Powell Lake. It was said if you looked at him, you would die.

Golden Stanley

# Olsen Valley:
## Memories of a Lost Community

Some people think the valley was named after the Olson family, and if it wasn't, maybe now it should be. The Olsons moved there in 1913 and were one of the first families to move into the valley. Olsen valley and creek are spelled on maps with the letter "e," but in newspapers and local writings the letter "o" is often used.

There are two other theories about how the valley got its name. One says that Olsen was a trapper in the valley and that he disappeared. Only his raft with a pack bearing his name was found. No one seems to know anything else about this man.

The other theory suggests that some student surveyors from Vancouver were so overwhelmed by the isolation and lack of culture that they named the place after a prestigious cultural family in Vancouver. As a joke, of course.

The valley, seventeen miles up Powell Lake, wasn't opened for settlement until 1910. This was the first time that homesteaders were able to get a title of ownership for a section of land if they cleared five acres. A section of land is 160 acres, and this procedure was called a pre-emption.

In modern days this sounds relatively simple, like free land. But in those days there was a lot of complaints about the terms under which the government gave title to the settler. Clearing five acres could cost the settler as much as $3,000; not to mention an incredible amount of hard work.

In 1912 Olsen Valley was burned out despite the efforts of two hundred fire-fighters, sixty-five of them from Bob Scanlon's logging crew.[1] They did save the stand of timber in Theodosia River Valley which eventually provided logging activities for twenty years.

Oren Olson, still a resident in Powell River, remembers when he and the rest of the family moved up to Olsen Valley. They came from Vancouver and stood wide-eyed at Powell Lake waiting for a boat. There were the parents and six kids: Bill, Gus, Pat, Peggy, Oren and Ray, the baby.

Oren Olson

Eventually they were picked up by a long thin gas boat that was called "The Toothpick." During the seventeen-mile trip up the lake Mrs. Olson became quite ill from the gas fumes. Oren remembers her lying down in another boat when they got to the landing. When they arrived several neighbours were there waiting to greet them and help them move their belongings four miles up a road and then three miles through thick underbrush on a primitive trail. In an interview with Mr. Golden Stanley, Harry Gothard recalled carrying a mattress for the new family. It took him from 7:30 in the morning until 8:00 at night. Oren remembers how they took the stove apart and carried it piece by piece on packboards.

The house they were going to live in was simple to say the least, and small, only fourteen by fourteen. Oren's dad made a tent for the boys to sleep in. He did this by erecting three-foot walls and a floor. Then he covered the top part with mill canvas.

The boys slept there for the first winter, and every night their mother would come and check to see if they were covered up and dry. By the second season Oren's dad had built two rooms onto the house. Oren's dad was a "tough Norwegian" and he accomplished an incredible amount that first year, clearing land, digging and planting two acres of garden, and setting up barns and fences for sixteen goats and one cow.

Oren Olson with the goats

The Olson children going to school

Home-life consisted of hard work and a few moments of relaxation in the evening beside a coal oil lamp. The Olson's could see mountain goats right from their kitchen window. They would come down into the valley for protection when it was stormy. In the spring there were lots of grouse and in the fall, bear meat was wonderful with "fat just like Crisco," Oren recalls. Oren's mother would use this fat to make berry pies. The garden produce up there was fantastic. Huge vegetables: turnips, carrots, potatoes and parsnips. Things like cabbage worms and aphids were non-existent.

In September the older boys took a six mile hike over to Theodosia Inlet. There was a 430 acre Sliammon reserve there called TOE-que-nun. This was a traditional village site that was abandoned in the 1920s. Some of the houses there were built on stilts because of the flooding. A good salmon stream flowed there, so it was a good place to get fish to take home to salt.

The Palmers had a beautiful ranch there, with forty acres of cleared riverbed land to raise feed for their herd of more than a hundred pure-bred polled angus cattle that grazed in the lush valley that stretched right to Olsen's valley. Sometimes the Olsons could hear the cow-bells from their place.

In 1912 one of the most exciting things that happened for seven-year-old Oren, was watching and helping the school being built. Everyone in the valley came to help, even the bachelors. There were fifteen families there: The Petersons, the Gishards, the Cristys, the Rowleys and the Rolandis, to name a few.

The Rowleys were from Saskatchewan and brought everything with them including cows, horses and pigs. Mr. Rolandi was "a good man with an axe" and built his house with hardly a nail, only dove-tail joints.

It took two months for them to complete the building of the school. It was all made of local cedar and only the doors and windows were brought in from Powell River. There was no insulation in the school, not even a ceiling, but there was a large stove that held thee or four logs at a time.

Oren's dad was on the school board and was selected to build the teacher's desk and the blackboard. "He painted the blackboard about fifty times and dried it behind the kitchen stove," Oren remembers.

Finally it was the first day of school. The Olson children, dressed in their best clothes, made their way down the trail to school. Oren's older brother was actually too old for school, but he stayed long enough to be counted so the necessary number of fifteen students would be met. Inside the school there were two long tables with benches. These were the children's desks. About three years later they sent some "regular" desks from Powell River, the kind with ink wells and metal legs that screwed to the floor. Looking back on it, they could have used the school for a community centre to hold dances in, but the desks being stationary, would have been a problem. And in those days schools were not used for other activities. The community never actually had a centre; people just met in each others homes.

The first teacher was Mr. Foley; he eventually went to war and was killed in action. After Mr. Foley, all the teachers were young women.

The teachers had to board with a family. Oren remembers that Mr. Norton and Mr. Shultz "got into a big row" because the teachers were always staying with Mr. Norton who was a jolly old fellow and lived close enough to the school that the teacher could go home for lunch. The school board was called in to settle the matter and it was decided that the teacher would stay one term at Nortons and one term at Shultz.

The teachers didn't make much in the way of money. "I bet if they made six hundred dollars a year they were doing good," Oren says. But the teachers all loved Olsen Valley. Maybe because of all the parties they had. As soon as the snow started getting heavy the parties began. There were two French men, Pierre Petit and Gus Chanson. Petit was a chef who used to cook on a luxury liner, and Chanson was an excellent wine-maker. They would supply all the food and drinks for the parties.

Chanson and Petit were proud of Marshall Foch who was the Commander-in-chief of the Allied forces of World War I. Foch proved to be a very skillful leader and was responsible for the vigorous pursual of the Allied Commanders joint plans.

When it came time to naming the Post Office, these two French men were so loved in their partisan approach that their suggestion prevailed and the name Foch was applied to the Post Office for Olsen Valley.

Mr. Knimps set up and ran the first Post Office until sometime during World War I, and then in the early 1920s the Post Office shifted location from the head of Olsen Lake to the Rowley house. In 1925, the Simards bought the house and took over the Post Office.

The second Olsen Valley school

The days at the first school were "a lot of fun." Oren remembers one day when the teacher was away at lunch, August Gilbert was doing hand-pulls from the rafter above the teacher's desk. The two-by-four broke and he fell and "sent everything all over the place. There was heck-a-popping when she got back."

In the winter when the weather was too stormy, the Olson children stayed with Mrs. Parks, Mr. Rolandi's housekeeper. Mrs. Parks had a little girl too young for school. She used to eat raw potatoes just as fast as her mother peeled them, but one night she got sick and died on the way to St. Luke's hospital in Powell River.

There was always at least two feet of snow in the valley during the winter. Sometimes when it was mild for a couple of days and then became cold again, the snow would develop a hard crust. The children would "run all over the country" enjoying the freedom from the usual trudging through deep snow.

In the spring the glaciers started melting and every year the Theodosia River would wash out the cedar bridge on Olsen creek. This was the bridge that the Olsons had to cross on the way to school. The men in the area worked on the bridge and the government paid them because it was a public road.

The melting snow also resulted in a major snow slide about a quarter mile from school. It would make a tremendous roar as it ripped down the mountainside. When that happened the children would run to the windows. "Now get back to work and never mind the snow-slide," the teacher would say.

Later on in the spring the teacher started a gardening project. The teacher dug up a square of land and the children were all piling rocks and digging. Each student had his own garden and everyone competed to have the best garden. In the good weather they would stay and work on their garden after school. Tom Plisson was the judge of the gardens. He gave five dollars for the best garden, two-fifty for the second and a dollar for the third.

All the children loved Tom Plisson. He looked like Santa Claus and was one of the best berry farmers in the country. He also owned a large boat and was responsible for taking the mail in and out, as well as serving passengers. He usually went out every Wednesday and returned on Friday.

When the weather became even warmer one of the noon-hour pastimes was to visit the Japanese at the shingle-bolt camp. Oren can still picture the Japanese, shading themselves with little mats on sticks while they ate their bowls of rice and drank their tea. They would always offer the children some of their lunch.

"At one point there were three shingle-bolt camps employing thirteen teamsters driving twenty horses, and nearly seventy-five Chinese labourers."[2] All were supplying bolts for shingles for Brooks-Bidlake shingle mill at the town end of Powell Lake or for Mowatt shingle mill at Mowatt Bay. These two mills "really lit up the sky at night" and they kept two tugboats going steady up and down the lake. After the first war the mill at Mowatt Bay closed down because after Olsen Valley wood had been used up there wasn't enough wood supplied along the lake to keep two mills going. Around 1917 the Brooks-Bidlake mill was bought by Doc

Jameson.

The Japanese had several shingle-bolt camps. In these camps they
would cut cedar and split them in halves or quarters in five foot lengths.
These were called bolts. In pre-war times they were paid fifty cents for
bolts and seventy-five cents for long bolts. The long bolts were sixteen
feet long. They used work horses to pull the bolts into Olsen Lake and
from there they were pushed down a flume to Powell Lake.

With all the work in mills available, Oren felt he must leave school
and make a living. He first started working with Robert and Walter Lasser
at their shingle-bolt camp "greasing skid."

Later on he left home to live with his brother-in-law Eli. At that
time Eli was trying to gain a title for his land so he could get a pre-emption.
All the homesteaders were faced with this awesome task of clearing five
acres of land. Some of the trees were four feet across, and the only
equipment they had to handle the job were axes, a cross-cut saw and a
hand-operated winch called a stump puller. Oren stayed helping Eli for
over six months clearing logs with an old horse.

In 1920 some inspectors told Olson he had cleared the wrong piece
of land. Naturally Olson was upset and demanded that the land be
surveyed. They said he had half an acre in the line, but they would give
him an acre and a half. Ole Olson was so angry he took his family out and
left almost everything behind, even the animals. They left in May 1920
and the lake was still frozen over. They went down to the United States
and bought a dairy farm.

They stayed there seven years before they came back to Powell
River. Clara Olson, Oren's older half-sister had married Andy Anderson,
and they were given a contract to log off the area which is now the Powell
River Golf Course. Clara asked her dad to come back and work for them.

When they came back they lived in town, but Oren wasn't long in
finding a way to visit the valley he loved so much. Things there had
started to change.

When the Olsons had left the valley there hadn't been enough
enrollments for the school to continue, so the first school had closed
down. In 1925 when the Simards moved into Rowley's place, enrollment
was up again and Mr. Simard donated an acre of land for a new school to
be built on. The first school was too far away because by then everyone
lived lower in the valley.

The Simard family had quite an impact on the valley. Mrs. Simard
ran the Foch Post Office and helped Mr. Simard run the strawberry farm.
Roger Simard has fond memories of their thirty-foot dug-out canoe,
three and a half feet wide with a four horse-power motor. This was the

same boat that brought the Olson family to Olsen Valley.

Roger remembers how they would load "The Toothpick" with strawberries to take to town to sell for twenty-five cents a basket, a good price in those days. Mr. Simard bought the farm for twenty-five hundred dollars, and with the strawberry sales, part-time work at the Paper Mill in Powell River, and a lot of help from his whole family, he paid for the place in three years.

Two deaths in the valley also created changes. Mr. Cristy had died in a logging accident, a cable had broken; and a couple of years later Mr. Rolandi married Cristy's widow. Rolandi sold his rights to Jack Harper and moved to Vancouver, and Jack used the place as a summer resort. People still talk about the way Jack used to drive his Model T right to the cabin door. His secret was "cedar punchings," cedar slabs, right over the swamp.

In 1927 Old Tom Plisson passed away and the Borer brothers bought his place. Originally they intended to run the farm like Plisson did, but they were offered a contract hauling logs for the Powell River Company. They did so well they never did farm the area but they did continue a boat service for the people of the valley. There were still some people there that had been there before though, the Nortons, the Baumons, the French men and still some great parties.

Logging in Olsen Valley

The most dramatic change in the valley was that "Merril and Ring" had moved in and logged off the old Olson homestead. They had started logging there about a year after Olsons left, and they kept logging until 1929. A lot of timber came out of there.

It was a locomotive logging show, running from Okeover Arm on Malaspina Inlet. They would haul all the logs down there and dump them in the ocean, boom them on high tide and tow them out to be used in Vancouver or Seattle. "They'd log everything into a spar tree, and then push the railway spur line in there, and when that was finished they'd pull up the steel and put it somewhere else," Oren explains. "They had their main camp at Okeover and in the morning the crew would go up to the valley by crummy, a railroad car with a house on it."

By the early '30s most homesteaders had moved away. The French men had both died of cancer and the Borers bought up their property as well. The house these two characters had lived in was little more than a shack so the Borers set a match to it. After the fire they found an old French money box among the ashes. They might have burned a fortune.

Only a couple families stayed until the '50s. These last residents sold some produce to the stores in Powell River, and worked at small logging operations on Powell Lake. The shingle market had declined and produce got harder and harder to sell in town as large food chains brought in fresh produce from outside sources. The rest of the residents sold their land either to a William Jamieson who realized that Powell River Company wanted the land and knew he would make a profit, or they sold directly to the company.

The last family in Olsen Valley was the Whitley family. They sold their property to the Powell River Company in 1954. With that purchase the Powell River Company owned the whole clover-shaped valley. Land that wasn't owned by homesteaders was bought from the government. The company wanted control of the valley so they could divert Theodosia River down through Olsen Lake. By controlling the diversion dam on Theodosia River the Company hoped they could guarantee a good water supply for the pulp mill in Powell River.

Jamieson, having sold his land holdings to the Powell River Company, also was granted the contract for the construction of the Theodosia River diversion. A low log crib dam was erected across Theodosia River and a quarter mile canal was built through to Olsen Creek. They estimated that the canal would be forty feet deep but it turned out to be a canyon a hundred feet deep. The total cost of the dam was approximately $250,000.[3] This added two thousand additional kilowatts of power for the mill.

The conversion dam destroyed most of the farms.

In the fifties and sixties the main activity in the valley was vandalism. People would take their kids there and let them "go to it." Many a Powell River adult remembers throwing desks out the school window, or smashing stair cases and French doors. "Hunting" parties were also a source of destruction.

In 1970 hippie squatters moved into what was left of Olsen Valley. A year later MacMillan Bloedel Ltd., the current owners of the pulp mill, told the squatters to leave. They said their woodstoves created a fire hazard.

After the squatters left, MacMillan Bloedel decided to burn down the buildings of Olsen Valley to discourage others from moving there. Only a few people objected.

The buildings were burned in 1972, and now there is little trace left of the community.

# Tom Ogburn

Originally from Kentucky, Mr. Ogburn, known as Tom, came to Texada Island around 1906. Four years later he arrived in Powell River in a rowboat with all his worldly possessions in a gunny sack. (P.R. News — November 19, 1931.)

He became a popular guide and lake enthusiast. Soon he established a hunting and fishing resort on Goat Lake. His float cabin, made of shakes and comfortably furnished, was on the shore of Goat Lake. It became a popular spot for hunting and fishing parties from Powell River as well as places further away.

Tom Ogburn had a Chinese cook who reputedly served trout for breakfast and lunch every day. Mr. Gordie Dycks who lives in Klahanie, remembers the cook well. "He saved my life," he says. Apparently young Gordie Dycks stole a cookie and the Chinese cook yelled at him. Gordie ran away and slipped and fell into the water. Luckily the Chinese cook could swim and dove after him.

Several years later Gordie saw the cook at a logging camp. "Do you remember me?" he asked. The Chinese cook just looked at him. "You pulled me out of the lake," Gordie reminded him. It was only then that the

Tom Ogburn's place: 1925

cook laughed remembering. He thought it was a great joke.

As late as 1920 it was not unusual to see a dozen deer from Mr. Ogburn's lodge. The hunters from Vancouver would bring the pelts down the lake and load them onto the logging train flat cars. The train ran from the townside of Powell Lake down along the Willingdon Beach Trail. The pelts would be unloaded at the corner of Second Street and Ocean View, where the Patricia Theatre is now. From there they would be shipped out by the proud hunters.

Mr. Ogburn had a tar-paper cabin located beside the railway in the middle of the present First Street. This cabin was moved here from the lake when the Powell River Company raised the lake in 1924. The cabin was decorated with totem poles and a sign across the front of the cabin read, "Everything from the Cradle to the Grave." Tom married late in life and while he and his equally aged bride were away on their honey-moon, some ingenious prankster covered "to the grave," and left only "Everything from the cradle."

Tom Ogburn lived until he was eighty-one years old. He died in 1931.

# Powell Lake Farm

In 1913, Mr. Van Bilderbeck was the first person to take a pre-emption on the land now known as Powell Lake Farm. The land is situated twelve miles up the lake and a mile or so back on an old logging road. A year-round stream runs through the property. The original pre-emption was 160 acres, but the Powell River Company bought off 80 acres.

The Van Bilderbeck family moved here from Florida where they had lived on a ten-acre orange grove. Originally from Holland, the family consisted of nine: the parents, five girls, one boy and a house-maid. They weren't there long when their house burned down, so they sold their property and moved to Vancouver. The house-maid stayed behind.

In Vancouver they decided to homestead on Powell Lake, but it turned out they never actually lived on the land. Instead they pitched their tent in a lovely grove of virgin trees on the old Cranberry Lake road. The tent was a circus tent, 33 × 17 which they had traded for seven Dutch bicycles in Vancouver.

At that time George Smarge was the telegraph lineman, and part of his job was to trouble-shoot the line from Powell River to Jervis Inlet. Soon after the Van Bilderbeck's moved in there was trouble on the line. Eventually Smarge found the problem. The Van Bilderbeck's laundry was hanging out on the telegraph wires.

The father worked in the mill as a tool repair man for Jimmy Kendrick. The boy of the family, Huubert, was working pushing drift-wood out of Powell River into a flume on the new dam. He started work as soon as he was thirteen. With both working it didn't take long before they were able to move into a company house on Cedar Street.

But soon there was more trouble. The company paid in scrip which could be used at the company store. When Van Bilderbeck's tried to save money on groceries by sending for them in Vancouver, they were repri-manded for not supporting the company, and eventually they were forced to leave. The family went to Lang Bay first and then to California. It seems they had better luck down south. As late as the sixties Huubert and his wife came to Powell River for summer vacation.

In 1915 Joe Errico was market gardening on five acres of townsite land which he had leased from the Powell River Company. He was supplying the town with most of its fresh vegetables. He also supplied firewood and had a huge reserve of wood behind his place at the edge of the woods. This is where a hot-air balloon landed and started a fire during the Dominion Day celebrations in 1914. There is a tennis court and bowling green on this site now.

"He was a fine little fellow," Curly Woodward remembers. "He spoke broken English, but that didn't matter. He sure knew how to make change and grow vegetables. He was an institution in the town. Everyone got a kick out of him because he neglected to put a period between the J and Errico, and everyone called him Jerrico."

After several years the company wanted to develop past the bowling green, and they gave Errico several offers for the land so he would break his lease. Errico didn't want to leave. Soon there were some strange things afoot and his place burned down. Errico used to protest about it and make flat statements about the fire. When he realized that the Van Bilderbeck's were moving he offered Mr. Van Bilderbeck fifteen dollars to release the pre-emtpted land on Powell Lake, and he moved up there with his brother and a cousin. They stayed pretty well to themselves when they lived there. The youngest man used to have a habit of crossing himself every time a stranger went by.

They made beautiful gardens there. Evan Sadler remembers going up there around 1926. "We got enough vegetables and melons to last eight of us for two and a half weeks, for only $2.50," he recalls.

They also grew grapes and tobacco. "We went into the attic in the house near Giovani Lake, and the whole attic was filled with tobacco leaves," Tony Mathews told me. The apple trees they planted are still on the farm. For irrigation they had a water reservoir which held about six hundred thousand gallons of water.

They tried to raise goats, but lost all of them one winter, and then tried sheep.

Stories of the Errico's are hard to find, but the late Art Lyons in a taped interview with Golden Stanley, related this anecdote.

Joe was complaining to Art about "Black Jameson" one day. (Jameson was the one who ran the shingle-bolt operations on the lake.) Art Lyons said to him in fun, "Why don't you shoot him? He's trying to steal your timber. Jameson always stands at the back of the boat, he'd make an easy target."

Well Joe thought about it and then replied in a very serious tone. "Oh no. I couldn't that. My mother wouldn't like it."

These Italians built a house that still stands, sort of. It is built near the stream and is set on a foundation of dug-in logs with hand-split eight by eight uprights every two feet. It is covered with a variety of hand-split

The house on Powell Lake Farm

logs, and covered again with hand-split shakes. The house was twenty by forty with two stories. Mark Vonnegut says, "The strangest thing about that house there wasn't a triangular brace anywhere."[4]

Eventually "Dago" Joe moved from "Dago Point" into Edgehill, taking his old horse Bill, with him.

Sam Spatari had the farm for awhile but didn't live there. The farm stood vacant for many years.

Then a group of young Americans who were disgusted with the Viet Nam war chose the farm as a place to escape in 1970. They couldn't believe their luck when they bought the place for twelve thousand dollars. The place was a "hippy's dream." They had wilderness, an unspoiled environment and a funky house that they made even funkier. There were usually about eight of them living there trying to be "good hippies." They managed to get a boat called "Blue Marcel" and a motor called "Goldy Moldy."

One of the first things they did was remodel the house by tearing off the roof and adding another story. After each trip to town the house gained another window. When they finally were finished "the damned thing looked like a pterodactyl learning to fly."[5]

Life on the farm might have been idyllic in some ways but for Mark life took on a night-marish quality. Isolation and insanity are often connected, thus the term "bushed." A visitor to the museum once told me that the phenomenon is related to the water. "Possibly the hemlock," he suggested. "Or maybe just the cedar."

"We guessed that maybe there was something in the water up there that some people's systems couldn't adjust to right away. But with me it was the other way. Every time I left the farm I seemed to get some sort of sickness," Mark Vonnegut writes in his book "The Eden Express." "Maybe I had become addicted to something in the water or air up there and my stomach problems when I left were withdrawal symptoms."[6]

Whatever the cause, Mark recovered and his book is interesting, not only because it recalls a trip into madness, but because it describes the feeling of being isolated near a "monster" lake, and it describes an age that is fast disappearing.

The last of the commune residents left the farm in the mid-seventies, but although they left the farm, they didn't sell it at first. One of the group, Peter Seixas, became a teacher at "Total Education," an alternate school in Vancouver. He saw the farm as an ideal site for a rural alternate school.

The Scheibers, Peter, Linda and their children, arrived to run the school that was designed to meet the needs of teen-agers who were unable to fit in or be motivated by the traditional school system.

The problem at first was lack of adequate housing. The farmhouse was hardly adequate but provided shelter while they were constructing new residences.

A huge log house which served as a boys' dormitory, and a girls' cabin were built about five hundred yards up the hill from the farmhouse. A pottery shed and kiln, a sauna and bath house, a solar-heated kitchen-dining room and a greenhouse were built by the children as part of their lessons. The goats, chickens, geese, ponies and two hives of bees encouraged the students to be responsible for lives other than their own. In the evenings Peter Scheiber and his students studied and dramatized "The Twelfth Night."

Eventually the school closed down due to the lack of funds. At the present time, 1983, the Scheibers lease the farm during the winter and spend only the summers there.

In 1981, 82 and 83 the farm was used as a site for a "Healing Gathering." People dedicated to the holistic way of living spent a few summer days at the farm.

# A Prospector's
# Memories

Billy Uzell (1876-1954) died the same year he wrote this article, in Oct. 1954. He was in Powell River in 1903 when the only inhabitants here were the Sliammon people and a logging outfit of Myrtle Point. The article was taken from the March 3 edition of *The Powell River News*.

In 1908, to get to the lake meant hauling your boat or canoe over the rough trail on the west bank of the river to the log dam. There was good fishing here. Up the lake to the large island was my first prospecting in that area. Failed to find anything of importance. I examined the island first, owing to the existence of a mineral claim some twelve miles up. This had been staked years before, a deposit of copper (Bornite) at the top of a high bluff. It looked inviting at first but there was no continuity. Many attempts have been made, in recent years, to develop this kidney of ore, but all have been abandoned. There was a camp of beavers there on the island, and they may still be there.

I did extensive prospecting, at various times, to a considerable depth, up the mountains at the head of the lake and towards Jervis Inlet. I was looking for gold and failed to find any.

At the right, upper point of the island is Goat River. This was full of boulders, so it was a case of pulling the boat up to Goat Lake, a bigger chore than getting one in from the salt chuck to the dam. Goat Lake was full of trout those days. My partner was quite a fisherman. I never did take to it. Up the lake on the east side, was a small creek and here was the best spot. Kept him busy pulling them in and I had quite a job getting him away. We established a camp here for our prospecting trip into the mountains.

Our objective was the range between the head of Goat Lake to Jervis Inlet.

At about 3,000 feet the rock formation was what is termed on the coast, the Vancouver series. It was fissured quite often, an ideal country for prospecting. Our sampling of veins and veinlets, on assaying, gave negative results of gold.

Our activities up there, which took up most of the summer were a distinct disappointment . . . There was no mineralization encountered, with the exception of a strong vein of Magnetite (magnetic iroin ore). This was over one hundred feet wide, could be seen running N.W. and S.E. for a long distance . . . it was a very interesting occurrence from a miner's point of view.

The failure to locate commercial ore was well repaid by the wonderful scenery.

At the foot of the Glacier we saw the largest congregation of deer and goats I have ever seen. There was a patch of green grass and other vegetation and that is what they were feeding on. There was a big Billy with them who seemed undecided whether to make a charge on us or not. The others just kept on nibbling and practically paid no attentin to us. Neither did we pay too much attention to them for there was just below us, a cliff. If William charged, it would be just too bad for us if he was not stopped. My partner and I held a council of war. We carried a carbine each. The result of the consultation was, if William lowered his head and prepared to charge, we would fill him full of lead. Our only way was to edge along the cliff for about one hundred feet and then it was clear going, so keeping our eyes on Billy, with our carbines at the ready, we commenced our crossing. Apart from shaking his whiskers he let us pass. There must have been over fifty deer and goats in that herd.

Lots of black bear were seen on this trip in the lowlands, but only one cinnamon and no grizzlies.

Coming out of the lake on this trip we found a large boat anchored at the mouth of the river. The owners who came ashore and found out where we came from asked if there was good fishing up there. We told them of the spot mentioned in Goat Lake. "Sounds good," they said, "would you care to go up with us. We will pay you well."

"OK," we said, "that's what we are looking for. Our treasury is about empty and the grub basket is very low."

Our boat was up at the dam as we had only brought our packs out. They looked like a prosperous bunch, there were four of them and we needed the money. They said they had plenty of food aboard, enough for a month if necessary. We suggested taking their small boat, that they had come ashore in along with us. The captain of the large boat was instructed to go to Blubber Bay, at my suggestion, for safe anchorage, and await our return. There were ladies aboard and they fell in with the plan but elected to stay with the boat and go to Texada.

Goat Lake was reached again and our old camp occupied. The men who were from Seattle, had the time of their lives for the fishing was better than they had anticipated. They also got quite a kick out of hauling the boats, etc. We stayed there about a week. One of them was a bank president, Scandinavian I think, and another was president-elect for the Yukon Seattle Exposition which was to be held in 1909.

When we got back to the mouth of the river, I rowed to Blubber Bay to notify the captain of the boat that they were waiting and ready to proceed up the Coast. Our payoff was $100 each and I received another $50 for the trip to Texada and we were given all the grub that was left over. I was guide on two more occasions up there, by a request from some friends of theirs, on the other side.

In 1941 I took the census of the people inhabiting the lake. Goat River had disappeared and there were so many changes that I hardly knew the area which I had known so well in the early days.

Before I leave the Powell Lake Area I would like to record another trip that I made up there. This time up the left arm of the lake and then up the river. I travelled alone with my little dog, Pickles, who was my companion on many trips that I made during the eleven years, off and on that I prospected up the lake.

Before my time on Texada, some Vananda miners had done development work on a copper deposit up the river. For some unexplained reason work ceased, although from two miners who had worked up there, I learned that it was a very promising outcrop. I failed to find it and as far as I know, no one else has located it.

I was up there about a month ago (February 1954) and found a quartz vein at about 1,000 feet above the bed of the river. Was busy sampling this when I heard a noise immediately above me. Glancing through the bush I saw a very big bear standing up, eating something. Thinking it was a black one, I gave a yell and told him to beat it and he yelled right back.

Figuring this was unusual, I took another glance and then I beat it. I probably went down that slide faster than anything that has ever been recorded. It was either a cinnamon or a grizzly. Anyway, whatever it was, it put the wind in me, for I was unarmed. Pickles must have sensed the danger too, for he lept ahead of me.

Pickles, by the way, was killed by a cougar some years afterward. Now reach for the salt.

There was a story in those days of a timber cruiser who got lost in the area of Powell Lake and Toba Inlet.

For days he had wandered about lost, with his food all gone. Fortunately he reached the river but was unable to walk or crawl any further. His dog Jack was in about the same condition. He said, "Jack, old boy, I guess this is the end." Looking at his dog for awhile he got an idea. "No," he said, "I can't do that to my old faithful chum. We will go together."

At last he thought there is a way out. "Come here Jack and lay beside me," he said. Jack did, so he promptly tied him up then cut off his tail, made some soup and gave Jack the bone. They reached the lake safely.

# Nick Hudemka
## Portrait of a Hermit

He was a gentle man, a man who lived in harmony with nature and believed in independence, self-sufficiency and hard work; but he was also a man who had many friends, enjoyed a party and nurtured a dream of finding the right woman, possibly a "fiery redhead," that would share his life with him.

The man was Nicodemus Hudemka, one of several hermits that lived in the wilderness just outside Powell River.

He left his home in Insinger, Sask. when he was only fourteen years old because, some say, his father was mistreating him. He escaped to the west coast and worked for logging companies in the Cameron Lake area. A couple of years later he went to Theodosia Inlet and worked for a logging company running a steam donkey. He received his steam engineering certificate and was very proud of it. When he was 34 the company closed down at Theodosia Inlet and in 1940 he made his way to Powell River.

By this time it was obvious to everyone that hand-logging was a good way to make money, but still it was a weighty decision; a solitary work with imperfect tools. No longer would Nick have his fellow workers noticing or encouraging him in his work.

Nick was issued the last hand logger license in British Columbia.

It was probably at this time that he made his clinker boat (the wood on a clinker boat overlaps on the side like a shingle roof) or possibly, being short of time, he bought it.

More than likely he puttered up the lake along the shore looking for a good "show" of superb timber.

Having decided where to select a claim Nick set about getting tools for his operation . . . a large saw, an axe, several heavy chains for chaining

Nick Hudemka

logs together, a light ratchet screw, a peavey and a large Gilchrist jack that weighed 100 - 125 pounds.

He packed up a sheet-iron stove and made sure he had a good supply of matches in tins. He probably packed flour and beans and bacon in a neat sack sewn up with oil cloth. He had his tobacco in boxes, and some canned milk and syrup. Knowing of the plentiful numbers of goats, bears and cougars — he took his rifle with plenty of ammunition. And he bought a few traps for trapping the smaller fur-bearing animals.

Once at the site, Nick camped in a tent while he built his cabin. First he cut a cedar log into eight and twelve foot lengths and split the straight-grained wood into planks. He made the house-frame out of poles and covered the frame with the cedar planks, put in a rough floor and made himself a bunk and a table.

Outside the cabin he made a small clearing and a shed — a place for his grindstone to sharpen his saws, and a place to store his wood.

The next thing to do was "hang the boom." This meant taking slim straight spruce logs, the longer the better — about 125 feet long, and boring four inch holes through each end of every log. The logs were then chained together so that it would stretch across the mouth of the bay. Anchored firmly to the shore on either side, the floating line of logs would give him harbour for the logs he cut. Once placed inside no logs could float out onto the lake.

He selected each tree to be felled with care because no one would hand log a tree unless he could sell it. Nick worked mainly on the steep side of the mountain because by law, a hand-logger is not allowed to use power tools. The trees on the shore, he felled directly on the beach. Those farther up the mountain would slide to the beach when felled directly down the hill. These trees were called "stumpers" and he would cut these trees first.

The trees still further up the hill were more difficult to handle. These he would fell across the slope to facilitate "bucking." The trees fell onto a cover of smaller trees cut in its path. These smaller trees kept the larger trees off the ground and served as "skids."

Once felled, the tree would be limbed and debarked on the slide next to the skids. The bucked log would then start to slide down on the skids, but whenever it was stopped by a stump or tree, Nick would have to free it by rolling it with a peavey or lifting the jammed end with a jack.

Like all hand loggers, Nick paid full royalty for the timber scaled, but no stumpage.

It would sometimes take Nick two weeks to get a single log down the side of the mountain into the lake. Still it would all be worth it, often producing a straight clean log 138 feet long with more than 8,000 board feet in it.

The work was heavy and dangerous. One time he was pinned under a log for twenty-six hours before he managed to free himself.

Nick used to give his friends a hard time about hunting. "The bears are my friends and they make trails in the bush for me," he went on. One friend remembers asking him "Did you ever have trouble with a bear?"

Nick said one bear came up for a couple or three days and he started thinking about it and he was getting mad, "and that bear came and it got me up a tree," he said, "and I was up that tree for several hours. I should have had my rifle." His hunting friends sure got a laugh out of that. Ironically, although Nick had little fear about bears, it is rumored that he was terrified of humming birds.

Another time Nick had trouble with a bear, he was heating some food in his cabin and a bear attacked him. Nick killed the bear and said that the attack was unusual. This bear was famished and since this happened in the middle of winter, the bear would normally be hibernating.

As the years went on, Nick built himself several cabins. There was the cabin at the head of Powell Lake. Here he planted root gardens and had a root cellar. He also had a float cabin at the head of Goat Lake, and one at the Second Narrows. Eleven miles back on Joan Lake, he had another cabin, built on land and he had a small garden here as well. There was another cabin on his trap-line two and a half miles up Daniels River. He used this cabin, but I was not able to find out if he built it.

Nick's diet was simple and easy to prepare; he ate canned goods and root vegetables and some venison.

He lit his cabins with gas lamps. Nick always kept clean clothes to come into town, but he did not have time to spend washing clothes. Every spring he would hang out his blankets to be cleaned and aired by the fresh mountain rain; a simple solution that worked.

At night Nick would listen to the radio and keep up with the world news. He particularly enjoyed listening to the talk shows. It was his company.

One of his friends remembers Nick visiting his cabin one night. Nick was kind of bushed from living alone and he said, "My radio's still on. I wonder what it's saying to me?"

In the winter Nick would follow his trap line, trapping mink and marten and some beaver. It took him a week to ten days to cover the traps.

Nick's float cabin at Second Narrows was close to the Rainbow Lodge. During the summer Nick would often work for the lodge supplying logs and repairing their diesel plant. He also kept a supply of old motors around to tinker with. He would keep writing letters for parts and when the company's patent ran out, only then would he resort to making parts himself on his forge.

Nick was well-known by fishermen on Powell Lake and enjoyed visitors. Every month or so Nick would come to the town of Powell River, and in his younger days he would go to Vancouver. For a hermit "he did things in pretty good style," comments Tony Mathews. If he wanted to go

48

to Vancouver or Seattle he'd go to Powell River and phone Powell Air. They'd land at his shack up the lake. He'd be there all dressed up and he'd jump in the plane. He used to go to Vancouver to see football games; he was a fan of the Lions. Some of his friends thought maybe he had a girlfriend in Vancouver.

Tony Mathews remembers coming down the lake and seeing Nick in his suit with his outboard on his knee taking it apart and fixing it out in the middle of the lake. He had an old "clinker-built" wooden boat. The boat, as time went on became hilarious, an antique. It took four hours for him to come down the length of Powell Lake. During his later years his friends tried to persuade him to buy a fibre-glass boat, but Nick refused saying a fibre-glass boat would never stand up the way his old boat did.

He was a good friend of the Rodmay owners, Al and Nilo Mantoani who delivered oil to him at his cabin near Rainbow Lodge, and who later looked after his supplies for him. He was also one of the few men who knew Billy Goat Smith well.

In the later years he suffered terribly from rheumatoid arthritis. Sometimes he was in so much pain he would stand in the cold waters of Powell Lake until his legs became numb.

The last three years of his life Nick was unable to carry on the strenuous hand logging he had been doing for thirty-eight years. His friends told him to take his money and buy a nice house in town, but Nick would have nothing to do with that idea. He would miss the wilderness, the silence of the mountains, the call of the loons, the bears, the eagles.

Nick's needs were very basic. His friends used to laugh and say that snuff was the only supply that Nick, by this time, Old Nick, could NOT do without.

His friends tried to persuade him to make a will, to leave his fortune to some charity — but Nick laughed them off. He would find himself that fiery redhead, marry her, and she would have his fortune.

The last time Nick came to town it was Christmas, 1976. He spent his time at the Rodmay and also at the private homes of Al and Nilo Mantoani. Don Hart rowed him back after Christmas along with some supplies.

On January 13, a man called the RCMP saying he had seen someone prone on a float at Second Narrows. That night Nick Hudemka's body was brought back to town on an RCMP vessel. He died of a massive heart attack when he was either entering or leaving his float cabin.

His obituary was printed in the *Powell River News:*

On January 12, 1976
Nicodemus Hudemka — at his residence on
upper Powell Lake, age, 71 years.

Funeral services Friday, January 16 at
3:30 p.m. from the chapel fo Stubberfields
Funeral Home. Cremation. Rev. A. Pike
officiating.

Later his friends took his ashes up to the float cabin at the Second Narrows. They held a memorial service for him there on the lake. His drinking buddies wanted to erect some kind of memorial for him, but it was one of those plans that was never executed.

His float cabin was auctioned by the government agent and Terry Foort bought it. The exact amount of his fortune is not known but it was estimated to be 350 thousand dollars. Because he had no known relatives, the government was the benefactor.

When I interviewed people for this article I was impressed by the affectionate way people spoke of him. "We miss him. He was a good friend," they said. "He was part of Powell Lake."

# Powell Lake Shingle Mill

The mill was built about 1913 by Brooks-Bidlake before a bridge was even built. During the years 1915-1916, a bridge was built at the foot of the present Cedar Street in Powell River. At that time the shingles were floated across the upper end of the river on a raft to the loading ramp; from there they were taken by rail down to Michigan Landing, now Willingdon Beach, and from there they were shipped off. Of course, a good many of the shingles were used locally because there was considerable house-building taking place. After the bridge was built the shingles were brought by truck or horse and wagon to the governmnent wharf which was inside the Powell River Company breakwater. Some shingles were shipped from the Powell River Company wharf.

Shingle mill on Powell Lake 1919

In the 1920s, Doc Jameson, a millionaire from Vancouver, bought the mill and continued to cut shingles there until 1953. Around the mill a town grew up at what now is known as the Powell Lake Marina. If you look around there are still a few traces of the settlement left.

In 1928 the community was a thriving town with about fifty houses adjoining the mill. They weren't the most modern houses in the world. There were one or two in fairly good shape, but the rest were more or less shacks. Most of the houses were rented by Japanese families, and the Chinese sawyers and packers stayed in their own bunk house. The mill supplied the houses with light, water and wood for fuel, until in the '30s they installed hot air heat. The water was pumped from the lake to a cement reservoir on top of the hill.

The mill also had an electric generator that furnished light and power to the mill and the houses. In 1928 about forty men were employed around the mill, most of them Chinese. The mill worked two eight-hour shifts. The Shingle Mill also employed seventy-five men in the woods at several camps up the lake. In 1928 there was a camp at Chippewa Bay, two camps near Goat Island, and two camps near the head of the lake. Besides the land at the Shingle Mill site, Jameson owned Mowat Bay.

The logs were cut into bolts up the lake. Bolts are logs cut into seven-foot lengths, and then halved and quartered. The logs were towed from the camps to the mill by tugs. At one time the company owned two tugs. The "Toklat" had a fuel diesel engine of forty-five horse-power and a speed of twelve knots per hour.

Once at the mill the bolts were carried up a conveyor belt to the cutting machines. In 1928 there were five cutting machines that cut the bolts into sixteen or eighteen inch blocks and then into wedge shapes.

From there the wedges were sent to the trim saw to have the edges squared off.

The sawyers always worked upstairs and when the shingles were cut they would throw the shingles down the chute to the packers, where they were sorted into two bins. Number one shingles went into one bin and those with small knots and imperfections went into another bin. The shingles were then packed together on a packing machine. Finally the packed shingles were put on an apron, and taken to the trucks. The trucks would take them down to the government wharf, Pier C, and loaded onto the scows.

In the mill itself cedar dust was a problem and most workmen wore small sponges over their noses.

Boats that came in for the Powell River Company would take a load of paper and carry shingles on the deck. "That was always quite a problem because we had our scows loaded with shingles down on the grid at the old government wharf, and at low tide they'd be sitting on the mud, so we'd have to work it so that when they were ready to take our shingles, we'd have the scows off the grid and ready to be towed alongside the ship," Chuck recalls. He remembers one time a ship called "The Tropic Sea" came to load thirty thousand bundles of shingles, and the ship started listing so they had to unload the shingles. There were shingles scattered all over Powell River Harbour.

The town also contained a steam laundry that was supplied with light, power and water from the mill. When the mill closed down the owner of the laundry was usually pretty upset. Chuck Wilcocks remembers Tom Yip being upset more than once.

At Sing Lee's store there was a restaurant with only four booths. The cook used to wait on the customers himself. They had rooms above the stores, but they were purported to have cockroaches so nobody slept there unless they had to.

Bill Gaston had a gas station on the lake. He was a pretty good mechanic and sold gas for boats and cars.

People who grew up at the Shingle Mill townsite remember the place as a natural playground. Living right on the water they were able to swim, fish or dive off the bridge. They could also pick berries or go for long hikes. However, there was always a lot of work to be done. Mrs. Oren Olson remembers gathering wood for the family with her sisters. Gladys Cockrill remembers staying with her brothers who had a piano to entertain friends.

One day in July, 1933 the local police received a call to come to the Shingle Mill. They found a bear on top of the framework of the bridge and a crowd of youngsters were watching the bear. As there seemed no safe way to get the animal back to the woods, it was shot.

Shingle mill on Powell Lake 1925

# Doc Jameson

Mr. Chuck Wilcocks, a resident of Powell River, worked for Doc Jameson from 1936 to 1942. Part of his job was to meet Doc at the steamship. Every Sunday morning at 6 a.m. Chuck would go into the ship's stateroom and meet him, and then a long day would start. After they got off "The Princess Mary" they would first go down and look at the scows that were loaded with shingles until the boats came and hauled the shingles away. From there they would go to the Rodmay and Doc, a man of habit, would buy them the same breakfast every week. It was always coffee and pancakes.

After that they would go up to the Shingle Mill and Doc would look at the shingle bolts that were brought in. At that time a lot of bolts were brought in by the local Indians. Chuck used to scale them. They'd be dumped into the water but sometimes if the scaler wasn't sure of the quality he would "rack" them so the scaler could tell how many there would be to the cord. Doc would always want to have a look. At the time they were paying about $5.50 a cord. Doc would shake his head and say, "They're not even worth five dollars."

"This went on a lot, but I got used to it," Chuck says.

Most Sundays Doc wanted to go and check the Shingle Bolt camp at Olsen Landing. Chuck would have to wake the operator, Bill Grafton, and drag him out of bed.

Grafton had often partied the night before and wasn't thrilled with the idea of getting up, but no one said no to Jameson. He'd get up half awake and still under the influence. Doc would turn to Chuck and say, "Has he been drinking?" And Chuck would say, "Oh, no. He's probably just not feeling too well."

They would all go up the lake to inspect the camp. And when they got back they would work at the office for awhile. Before he was married, Chuck had a room at the back of the office and Doc would go to Sing Lee's store and buy all kinds of food, and come back to Chuck's kitchen to cook it. Doc was a vegetarian and "he'd make some awful concoctions. He'd take a cucumber and stuff it with peppers and mushrooms and cook it in the oven."

It was a long day before Doc Jameson was ready to return to Vancouver on the 11:15 p.m. ferry.

There were several shingle-bolt camps during that time. There was one at Olsen Landing that was run by Jameson, and the other camps were operated by Japanese and Chinese. There was one Chinese man, a great big fellow, who was boss of the camp at Goat Lake. That camp is all grown over now. Doc would pay them so much a cord. There were two or three other Japanese camps; one fellow by the name of Kowakita, used to come down and do physical exercises in front of the office, "drunk as a skunk," Chuck remembers.

Before Chuck worked for Doc there was a shingle-bolt camp at Bear Tooth. They decided to re-open the camp because there was a lot of shingle bolts left lying in the upper slopes.

Doc phoned Chuck one day saying he found some good workers for the camp, and he brought them up with him from Vancouver. Within a week one had fallen off a flume and broken a leg, and they were all on compensation within a month. Of course compensation wasn't as much as it would be now.

Old Sam Sing, who ran the store died in Powell River. Doc was an old business aquaintance of his; "they worked for or against each other for a long time." When Doc heard that Sam Sing had died he called up Chuck and said, "I'll be up for Sam's service and I want to have something read at the church . . . I'll make up something and you can type it out when I bring it up there." When the day of the service came Doc had his message read and turned to Chuck and saying, "That sounded pretty good Chuck, didn't it?"

After the service they had a funeral procession through the Shingle Mill, and all along the way there were fire-crackers and fire-works being set off.

They were non-union employees at the Shingle Mill. Doc brought in some white sawyers and packers: Charlie Little, and his two sons. Also George Cameron and several others. Charlie, who was about sixty when he came to the mill, had been a shingle weaver for a long time. Most of the men who worked in the mill were Chinese. The mill ran two eight-hour shifts for years, but for a short time they ran three shifts of seven hours each.

It was Doc's idea to have the houses at the mill site heated with steam. "We laid the steam line all the way from the mill, over to the office first to try it out, and that worked, so we took the line up to the houses. It worked pretty well when the mill was running," Chuck remembers. Doc didn't charge any of the tenants for the heat.

At one time the orders were slack and instead of closing the mill down they stacked them down by the water. At one time there must have

Jameson's Shingle mill

been sixty or seventy thousand bundles stored there.

"He was a remarkable man," Chuck recalls. He was a husky man with a "yellow" skin. A wild rumour said his mother was an Indian Princess."

One night Chuck and Doc were working in the office and Doc told Chuck to take one of the counters and hide it for him. So Chuck went outside and walked around the back. He had no light and it was absolutely dark. Chuck had a little garden back there and he hid the counter under a plank. When Chuck came back Jameson went outside, knocked on his head a couples of times and went straight to the plank in the garden. "I don't believe that stuff, but I saw it," Chuck says.

No one knows why he was called Doc. If you asked him he changed the subject. The rumour was that he had been a doctor in the States. In any case, he was a smart man and was worth a lot of money and he made a lot of money from the shingle business on Powell Lake.

# The Toklat

The tug-boat that belonged to the Shingle Mill was called the Toklat and Bill Grafton was the skipper. He would chug up the lake to get a tow of shingle bolts and take them back to the Shingle Mill. Sometimes they'd just be cutting the last shingle bolt in the pond, with the new boom out in the water being scaled.

Chuck Wilcocks remembers one time when Bill was so tired he fell asleep while the tug was operating. He landed up on the shore on the way down the lake. Some hours later he woke up. It was a diesel tug and it was still chugging away and not going anywhere when he was having a sleep. The people at the mill thought he must have had an accident and were about to go and look for him. They were sure glad to see him coming around the point.

Another day when Mr. Wilcocks and Mr. Jameson were going up to Olsen Valley with Bill, they had to load on about two dozen kegs of nails. Bill accidently dropped a fifty pound keg of nails off the wharf and into the water.

One morning in 1941 when Chuck was going out to scale Bill came over and said, "Well I guess we don't scale today. I haven't got the tug. You'll have to come over to the wharf. You can see it but that's about all."

The "Toklat" had sprung a leak and was sitting at the bottom of the lake right off the wharf. The forty foot tug had not suffered great damage but Bill lost a radio, blankets and other personal effects as well as a large quantity of food.

Of course it was Chuck's duty to report the incident to Jameson. "I phoned him, and you could see the sparks flying over the phone," Chuck recalls. Burg and Johnson came over with cables and cranes and were able to raise the tug by the end of the day. The boat and engine all had to be dismantled and cleaned before it could work again.

In August of 1942 Bill Grafton met with more adventure. The tug was in the open water off Cassiar Island when he heard a terrible bang. "When I looked up there was a hole two feet square over me. It looked just as if we'd hit a snag, but there isn't a thing in that part of the lake. It must have been lightning," Bill reported to the Town Crier. The mysterious explosion tore a chunk off the top of the wheel-house of the tug.

Probably the person who was happiest to see Bill Grafton was

Joseph Borer of Olsen's Valley in 1944. That April Joseph Borer struck a submerged log with his thirty foot gas boat the "Vernu." Before the craft went under water Borer managed to swim to shore where he lit a fire and spent the night and most of a Tuesday hoping that someone would spot him. He was stranded there for fifteen hours before Bill Grafton came to the rescue. With Borer aboard, the "Toklat" proceeded on to Olsen's Landing and returned later along with another tug to help re-float the "Vernu." She was towed to the landing and beached for repairs.

When the Shingle Mill closed down in the early fifties, the "Toklat" was taken off the lake and worked a few years out on the "chuck." Henry Pavid remembers seeing her out there during the fifties.

# The Laundry

Sing Lee was one of the first merchants here. His store was near the old central building and was in competition with the company store. Above the building they had rooms to rent for the single men. Other stores in the building were Somberton's, Wilshire and Lant, and a pool hall run by Steele. This pool hall was later run by Jack Harper. There was also a dentist, a Mr. Morrison, and a Star restaurant. This was also the first location of Fifth Avenue Dress Shop which was run by a Miss Wales who later became Mrs. Loukes. She still runs a dress shop on Marine Avenue.

The Sing Lee Laundry was down near the shore south of the company dock. It was a typical Chinese laundry. Everyone was given a ticket with some Chinese calligraphy on it and people used to puzzle over what it said. It was not your name but a description of what you looked like. "No tickey, no laundry," was the rule.

The company decided they needed the property to expand their store, so they bought the Sing Lee Block and Sing Lee moved south of the Shingle Mill and stayed there several years.

On December 12, 1928, a huge fire broke out near the Shingle Mill at the laundry. It started around 10:30 p.m. There was a strong wind. Imagine the Chinese workers running back and forth speaking excitedly in Chinese. Imagine them manning the Shingle Mill's two-inch fire hose only to find that there was insufficient pressure, just a slight trickle of water coming out of the hose while the flames raged up around the laundry.

For two hours it looked like the whole townsite area of the Shingle Mill would be burned down. Finally the Powell River Company's new fire truck came to rescue the place. The firemen jumped out of the truck with their thousands of feet of four-inch hose. But by the time the new fire engine arrived over the terrible roads, the fire was well under way and there was so much slush and water it was hard to even get close to the action.

Eventually the fire was controlled, but the Sam Lee Steam Laundry and the two bunk houses were completely destroyed. The Sam Lee Company loss was twelve to fifteen thousand dollars, but was covered by insurance.

It wasn't until April 1929 that a new steam laundry started up operations again. At this time the business was taken over by C.W. Steeves and Emile Gordon. The new laundry was a large frame building sixty by seventy feet.

The power for the steam laundry was furnished by a twelve horse power steam engine which used steam from the boilers of the Shingle Mill. The boilers there used refuse from the mill as fuel. As a result, the steam was generated at a low cost, the disadvantage being that when the Shingle Mill closed down the laundry went out of operation as well.

The laundry also had a ten kilowatt generator for electricity that they could use for power that they needed for light, washing machines and irons.

The new laundry had four large washing machines; a small one used for individual and delicate work, and the other four used for larger items. For hand-ironing there were six ironing boards with paper-covered troughs underneath.

There was a sorting room and a drying room. The laundry was collected from the residents in a covered van. When it arrived at the laundry it was first sorted and each group of clothes would be washed separately.

After being washed, the clothes went to the large flat ironer or to the drying room. This room was heated by the hot air and the clothes to be dried were hung out on large wooden horses. The wet clothes were wheeled in and wheeled out when they had reached the proper drying stage.

At that time the newest piece of equipment in the new laundry was the "centrifugal drier" described in the Powell River News as "a machine with a perforated inner cylinder which turns at a rapid rate of speed, throwing the surplus moisture into the outer cylinder, from where it passes to a drain."

After being ironed and folded the clothes were sent back to the sorting room, where they were checked with the original list, and parcelled for delivery.

In 1929, the laundry employed eleven local women and represented an investment of approximately $15,000.

The laundry was later sold to Tommy Yip who operated the laundry for seventeen years and then it was sold to Bill Pilling in 1946.

# Emile Gordon

One of the men who owned the Laundry in 1929 was Emile Gordon. Emile was one of the old Yankee traders, an entrepeneur. Originally he ran the Powell River Company store, but he was "let go" and a man named Merrick replaced him. After that Emile went into so many businesses that no one can remember their sequence. At one time he took over the bakery which used to be down near where the Steam Plant is now. He ran the bakery for a considerable time before he took over the shoe-making business on the front street that was made up of tar-paper shacks. Then he went into the cork picture-framing business. For a while he worked at a little mill cutting wood and selling it, and then he went into the car business. At the same time he had a store in the Rodmay. First it was a musical instrument store and then it was a radio store.

Jim Hukster worked for Emile. One morning when he came into the store Emile said, "Do you know anything about refrigerators?" Jim said no. "Well you'll have to learn fast because I'm going into the business," was Emile's quick reply. Jim was re-educated about thirty or forty times.

There is a well-known story circulating about town still. It is the story about Bob Foote. When Emile was in the car business he had a man from out of town comment that he sure liked that car in the Powell River Company's parking lot. "I can arrange that for you," Emile said. And without any sort of permission, the fellow got the car. They used to leave the keys in the car, so the happy customer hopped in the car and drove off. Luckily Bob Foote, who had no intention of selling the car, was satisifed with the price and went off and bought himself another one.

One time Emile sold a car to a man from Texada Island and he took a cow as part payment. He hitched it to the tree in front of the Rodmay. The cow was eating all the grass and the owner of the Rodmay, "Bat" MacIntyre looked out and the cow was eating the flowers. MacIntyre ran down the stairs yelling, "Emile, get that damn cow out of here!" So Emile had to get rid of the cow.

Emile took a lot of things in trade, old stoves and machine parts. During WW II all scrap metal was going to the war effort and stoves were hard to get. Emile had a barn full of stoves and things out in Westview, and when he sold them he made a fortune.

"I'm sure he could sell refrigerators to Eskimos," says Curly Woodward, one of many people who has fond memories of this outrageous man. After he died, Gordon Avenue was named in his honour.

# The Japanese Internment

Originally the Japanese came to the west coast as cheap labour. Most of the Japanese became Canadian citizens because that could be obtained in Canada without too much trouble, but the immigrants and their children were not allowed to vote. Not having the vote hurt the Japanese Canadians in many ways; for example, no one could become a lawyer or pharmacist in British Columbia unless he was on the voter's list.

The Japanese had some shingle-bolt camps up Powell Lake. Their camps were characterized by their little cooking boxes filled with gravel in their sparsely furnished shacks. The owner of the shingle mill would buy bolts from them, and like most businessmen of the time, Jameson paid them less than they deserved.

There is very little record of the activities in the Japanese shingle-bolt camps. Only the tragedies were reported in the local newspaper. From these tragic reports we know that H. Nakamura had a camp at the head of the lake near Bear Tooth Creek.

On May 6, 1935, there is a record of the drowning of a Japanese boy, Mitsuru Endo. The local police were notified and investigations revealed that the seven-year-old child was playing on the raft on which the family's cottage was built. H. Nakamura pulled the body from the bottom of the lake with a pike pole; and he tried artificial respiration without success. The family had only been there for a month.

On May 21, 1936, there is also a record of Soo Jan Kee, a forty-five year old Chinese cutter employed by H. Nakamura in a shingle bolt operation at McMillan creek. This unfortunate man met instantaneous death when he fell off a flume into a rocky creek. Later a jury of six men decided that it was an accidental death with no blame attached, but recommended a guard rail be erected on the edge of the flume.

The end of the Japanese shingle-bolting activities came after 1941 when war was declared between the two countries. In 1942, the Canadian government decided to evacuate all Japanese Canadians along the B.C. coast. At the time the government officials felt the internment was justified because they felt the Japanese could not be trusted and thought if a Japanese invasion occurred that the Japanese here would know the bays and inlets and could help invaders. The officials made no distinction between the Japanese from Japan, and the Japanese from Canada. Although many Japanese men were willing to fight for Canada, only a few were admitted into the army later on. The atmosphere of suspicion and mistrust, and the fear that the public safety was at stake made the removal of the Japanese seem imperative at that particular time.

"Now people misunderstand what was going on," one oldtimer states emphatically, "But it was a pretty tense situation. Before Pearl Harbour, the Japanese from Japan used to be out here taking soundings up and down the coast. I even had Indians tell me that they were talking to them saying how good they'd be to them when they came here. During the Pacific war Japan sent over hot air balloons and tried to set the forests on fire. They also shelled one of the big lighthouses on Vancouver Island. They later occupied the Aleutian Islands and were in a very threatening position to attack the whole Pacific Coast of North America. We felt very vulnerable here, although York Island had guns to guard the entrances coming into this area."

A Reserve Army was set up in Powell River to protect the town. They had practice exercises between Comox and this town where they tested the security of the town and the major industries. One night they tried to see how vulnerable the mill was, and the Oriental commandos training at Comox came over in the dark of night, and within half an hour they had all the armed watchmen tied up and were in complete control.

Another time they staged a night attack on the dam. The officers and the N.C.O.'s of the Powell River S.C.O.R.'s, a rifle company, were all there to watch for this commando Trainees group. "It was dark and we were listening, listening, and by God, the Bofor guns, anti-aircraft guns with blank charges just started with a concerted bang, and these things were coming over the dam about twenty feet over us. The first thing we knew there were three inflated boats coming right up the dam. You couldn't hear a sound coming down that hillside; they came down, no trails, and were so silent, so well trained. And they were dead on with those guns too; they were firing them off the big scow. We were really surprised and so were the suddenly-awakened sea gulls which in their panic were so disoriented that they flew upside down and backwards. It was really frightening to think how much more vulnerable we would be if this were a real attack."

Home Front: 1939-45

Regarding the internment of the Japanese on this coast, another resident explains. "I don't think the government had any alternative. They had to leave them all here, or put them all out. It was a case of a lot of innocent people suffering because of a few militant Japanese."

There were about twenty Japanese who were removed from the shingle mill. The men were mostly sawyers and packers.

"The Japanese we had here were a pretty good lot, and I especially remember a young boy, Jim Nakatsu, a boy about eighteen," recalls Chuck Wilcocks. "You couldn't meet a nicer boy. He was born out here, but he had to go with all the rest of them, and I remember another Japanese, a kindly old fellow, Nehemi Mahara, and he wouldn't hurt a bug. There was a young girl there about seventeen, and she came over and gave me her radio. She couldn't take it with her so she wanted me to have it. She came over to the office and gave me that radio. I used it several years. It was very moving to see them go. Mrs. Kinishi was the barber at the shingle mill. She had her chair right in the front room, in her parlour and the people would come in from all over, not just the shingle mill."

The Japanese in the shingle-bolt camps were single or just didn't have their families with them, but the ones at the mill had families. Mahara was a bachelor, but the others, Masutis, Knishis, all had wives and children.

It was March 19, 1942, that the Powell River News announced the "Jap Exodus Completed." The last to leave were from the Stillwater area.

"This completes the rounding up of 119 Japs in this immediate vicinity and a total of over 200 in the Powell River district extending from Pender Harbour to Toba Inlet. Not a Japanese man, woman, or child remains in this area . . . nor even a Japanese canary. With Wednesday's exodus one Jap was observed fondly carrying the family canary, cage and all."

The scene of the Japanese standing on the wharf with the police, and one-way tickets in their hands was a poignant picture which roused the sympathy of most residents in Powell River.

None of the Japanese families ever returned to live in Powell River. They were sent to road construction camps in the interior of B.C., detention camps in abandoned mining towns in B.C., or sugar beet farms in the prairies. Those who were considered troublesome were sent to a kind of prison camp in Ontario.

In 1944, the Japanese Canadians were told that the government would be willing to pay their way to Japan after the war. They were encouraged to find homes and work east of the Rockies. It wasn't until 1949 that they were allowed back on the coast.

As far as I know, Jim Nakatsu was the only person who returned to visit his former pals at the shingle mill. In spite of obvious hardships he managed to become a child psychiatrist and is presently operating a successful business in Ontario.

# Fires at the Shingle Mill

People who remember the Shingle Mill associate the place with fires. "There was always a fire down there," they say. After the fire at the laundry in 1928, there were several other fires.

On April 30, 1931, the second major fire at the Shingle Mill occurred. This time the mill itself burned down, and several houses as well. Even though it was out of their limits, the Fire Department from Powell River came to the scene.

There was considerable mystery surrounding this fire. The editor of the local newspaper was refused information about the fire. Many people speculated that the reason for the fire was obvious. This was 1931, a depression year. The markets were down and the Shingle Mill had insurance. "I don't know how Jameson got away with it," one old-timer complained; however, there never was any proof that the fire was anything other than accidental.

Another major fire was reported in the Powell River News in April, 1945. Fire started from a spark in the middle of the night. A diesel unit that was used for lighting and water pumping was totally destroyed. Insurance of $2,000 was held on the equipment. An adjoining building owned by Harold Allman escaped with $500 worth of damage. If the Powell River Fire Detachment had not come to the scene, Harold Allman's building would have been burned as well.

Since the diesel unit was destroyed, the mill residents were without electric light on Sundays and after the mill-operating hours. Water supplies were able to continue.

When Harold Allman, who was the mill manager at that time, was called to the fire in the mill, he leapt out of bed and tackled the fire with a large extinguisher. But when the wind caught the fire it lighted up an oil tank. "I just had time to shut off the outfit and get out when an explosion was heard and a forty-five gallon coal oil drum went sailing through the air," he said.

The lath mill in the adjacent building owned by Mr. Allman, was shut down for a day while they replaced belting and tools that were stored in the diesel house.

The next major fire occurred in November of 1950. Fire struck the

Shingle Mill structure again and this time a truck and garage owned by R.H. Goffin were damaged. The blaze was reported to have started from an acetylene torch.

In February 1951, the saw and planer mill were razed. As a result, the community was without electrical power because the diesel-powered generator which supplied the houses was destroyed. The pump which supplied water to the dam from the lake was also destroyed.

The mill was not operating at the time of the fire but the pump was, and the fire probably started from the motor. It was checked only a few minutes before by William Wheeler who said everything appeared to be in order. In this fire, none of the loss was covered by insurance.

The Powell River Fire Department was called in, but this time it was too late. The building was tinder dry and the only part they managed to save was the corner of the mill where the planer was located. Belts were burned right off the planer, but with new belts, the planer was able to operate again.

James Martin lost his car in the fire. As well as that, 25,000 feet of lumber was lost. The pump and generator were owned by Mr. Jameson.

In 1951 the Powell Lake Shingle Company, along with its townsite and logging interests were sold by J.F. Jameson to the Olsen Creek Logging Company.

The president of the purchasing company, George O'Brien, expressed that he had grave doubts about the continued operation of the Shingle Mill, saying it was not an economical operation at the time. The Powell River Company bought the Shingle Mill in 1953. John Galoca tore down most of the houses for lumber. After the Shingle Mill burned down there was no way of getting power or water to the houses, so most people moved out.

The parts of the Shingle Mill that hadn't burned down were salvaged for the arena on Marine Avenue which was built by volunteer labour.

# Ray Sims

The year was 1950. The date was August 2, a hot summer day. On your doorstep that morning you might have found a Powell River News. If you had picked it up and glanced at the front page, the first thing you would have noticed would be a picture of a wrecked airplane, the Diotte Cessna 140 which had crashed six days before, on July 27. The plane in the photo looked as frail as a dented tin can. As your eyes carried on over the page, you might have read the headline: Local Pilot Loses Life in Plane Crash at False Bay, and then you would have noticed the picture of the pilot, Ray Sims, a young man of only thirty-three years. He was a popular person, especially in the Shingle Mill site where he lived, and everyone was shocked by his sudden death and extended sympathy to his young widow and seven-year old son Ronnie.

The accident happened about 2:30 in the afternoon, just after Sims picked up his Lasqueti Island passenger who was coming to Powell River to visit her husband Manford Cook who was in the hospital with a broken leg from a logging accident. The plane was in the air only a couple of minutes after the take-off from False Bay when it suddenly slipped sideways and dropped into the water.

An eye-witness to the fatality, Charles Williams, stated that the plane was about three hundred feet in the air when it suddenly fell. He said the engine didn't stop, the plane just seemed to roll over on its side and fall.

The plane was completely demolished. The wreckage was picked up by the "Fort Ross" and brought to Westview wharf and later taken to Powell Lake.

At the time of the accident, no planes were available in the district and an ambulance plane of Associated Air Taxi in Vancouver flew to Powell River to pick up Dr. D.R. Collins and William Diotte and transport them to the scene. The plane later returned with the injured woman.

Sgt. D.R. McWhirter and Skipper Nelson Winegarden were flown to False Bay by a provincial police plane to conduct dragging operations.

Examinations of the wreckage revealed that the catch of the single safety belt had broken under the strain when the plane struck the water. Probably the weight of the two passengers against the left door forced the door open and the pilot fell out into the water. Mrs. Cook was able to crawl out and cling to the wreckage. She was picked up by the crew of a fishing boat which was about three hundred yards from the scene.

The Inspector of the department of transport came to Powell River to investigate the cause of the accident.

Friends of Sims, particularly those who had flown with him were shocked by the accident as he had a reputation of being particularly skilled and careful, and he was a very experienced pilot. He had served with the RCAF, flying Spitfires with a fighter squadron. In 1944 he was shot down over Holland and for six weeks was reported missing while he lived with the Dutch underground. Eventually he was freed by advancing troops. In 1948 Sims went into partnership with W.J. Diotte and formed the Diotte Airways Limited. As well as carrying passengers they also helped in fire-fighting; for instance in May of 1948 Ray Sims flew in two fire pumps and 3,000 feet of hose during a forest fire at Goat Lake.

A special memorial service was held in St. Paul's Anglican Church on Thursday evening, August 3, in Powell River.

As to what exactly happened in that accident, we will never know.

# The Andersons

Christened Amandus Ephraim, Andy moved to America from Sweden when he was four years old. His father had fourteen children from his first marriage and nine from the second. It is said he was the first fur-farmer in Wisconsin.

Andy's first winter in Canada was spent at Cold Lake, Alberta, trapping for the Hudson Bay Company. In 1901 he came to B.C. and was a log contractor at Nelson, B.C. where he was well known because he had a pet bear. Seven years later he moved to Powell River and declared "I'm going to stay here 'til Hell freezes over." Here he started cutting railroad ties for a railway line working for Michigan and Puget Sound Lumber Company on Powell Lake.

In 1908 Powell River only had a population of about fifty. Andy started logging on his own and getting his own logging contracts. He met Clara at Olsen Valley where she was living in a little cabin on Powell Lake.

Clara was a liberated woman long before the Women's Liberation Movement began. At a time when other women of the day passed their time with needlepoint and finery, Clara was out hunting. Her father, Ole Olson spent many a sleepless night worrying about his tomboy daughter. The clothes she wore — pants, headbands and men's boots — were unheard of in those days.

Andy and Clara were married in 1927 and made quite a team. Both loved the outdoor life and hunting, and both could drive the logging trucks. They lived in a plain house simply furnished with guns, goat and bear-skins.

Andy soon got a contract to log off the golf course. At one time he owned sixty-two lots in Powell River and supplied lumber to build houses on them for the Powell River Company, but during the depression like everyone else, they went broke.

In 1932 they started their own mill on Powell Lake, the Lakeview Lumber Company. He bought the sawmill in Cranberry from Marlatt and operated on land which was leased to them from the Company at Haywire Bay. Clara had a running feud with The Powell River Company, and used to plant corn down the middle of the road so the Company trucks would have a hard time travelling the vicinity.

Being a quiet sort of man, Andy left the office work and "public relations" to Clara, (also spelled Klara, Claire and Klaire). She didn't mind suing people, and more than once supreme court action was taken against her for damages incurred during malicious prosecution.

Clara Anderson — 1925

In 1938 Andy and Clara expanded their operation by purchasing a 110 horsepower steam engine and a new cutting machine. This doubled the power and cutting capacity of the mill. Everything in the mill was steam-driven. Over the years they bought equipment from Wasat and Mowat's Shingle Mill which was the shingle mill at Mowat Bay, and they bought other equipment from the Carter Brothers in Vananda, and the old Hasting mill in Vancouver.

When the union movement became strong Clara did her best to avoid the whole thing. In May 1946 when the coast loggers went out on strike, Clara made the following statement to The Powell River News: "Lakeview Lumber Company, not being a union shop, will continue operations until forced to shut down. We are particularly anxious to keep operating due to the need of ex-servicemen for lumber to build homes."

Andy Anderson

In June 1946, the following report appeared:

"Lakeview Lumber mill has been a thorn in the side of the local strike committee ever since the strike started on May 15. The owner, Mrs. Clara Anderson refuses to have anything to do with the IWA and has continued operations despite the strike.

"Two weeks ago picketers trailed a truckload of hot lumber from her mill to Lund, and were about to prevent unloading of the truck when Forest Ranger Yinling called them out to fight a fire."

Talk about Luck!

"I was over by the Wildwood bridge picketting Clara Bell's mill during that strike," one man recalls. "It was worth your life to picket because she'd run right over you. We were all young then. We thought it was a big joke. We'd stand there with our picket signs and she'd come with a load of lumber, and as soon as she got close to us she'd tromp on the gas and drive past about fifty miles an hour. The picket line didn't mean a damn thing to her."

The Lakeview Lumber Company carried on a torrid operation for twenty-eight years until the Company Lease expired in 1960. They moved the entire mill to the sixteen acre property on Mowat Bay, the place where they had lived for years. The mill never worked again because the municipality wouldn't allow them to run the operation at that site.

Andy was never short of things to do even after the mill closed. He kept active hunting, fishing and working on his Powell Lake booms salvaging logs.

"I met Andy one time when I was out hunting mountain goats," one acquaintance told me. "He was a hunter and he hunted all his life. He used to feed his logging camp with deer meat and goat meat and whatever he could shoot. But he was getting on when we met him up in Olsen Valley, and he was coming out with a goat in a wheel barrow, coming down the logging road. He must have been in his seventies then."

In September 1975, Andy was going out on his booms when he fell out of the boat into the lake. He hung onto logs for two hours before he was rescued. "I'm cold as a toad," he grunted when they pulled him out of the water. He was in his eighties then, and so strong that he only had to stay one night in hospital after being in the water so long.

"He used to talk about the harmful effects of white sugar," his friend tells me. "If that was the answer he sure was a big strong man right to the end."

In 1976 the Heritage Village bought Andy's entire stock of mill equipment, and it may be seen at Burnaby's living museum still.

Andy died in 1977 at the age of 87 years. A graveside service was

Anderson's mill

held at the Powell River cemetery. His wife Clara presently resides at the hospital in Powell River.

# P.R. Lockie

No history of Powell Lake would be complete without mention of P.R. Lockie who climbed most of the mountains around the lake. Lockie and R.H. Simmons were the first to climb to the summit of Bear Tooth Mountain on July 21, 1935. They had made two previous attempts and were stopped by heavy rainstorms both times. Lockie was also the first one to do the snow survey for the Powell River Company in 1938. A mountain is named after him: "Lockie's Table."

P.R. Lockie was a different sort of person; he either liked you or he didn't. He was direct and if he thought a person was being phony, he would have nothing to do with them. Because he treated everyone with complete honesty, he expected the same in return.

"I've often thought of a quotation I saw recently about someone else," says Graeme McCahon. "It said he was all crocodile on the outside and pure marshmallow within. That's rather how P.R. was."

P.R. was a teacher first but his direct way of talking to children was not approved of by the religious principal of Brooks at the time. "Enough Lockie-talk" was what was said. Lockie became a life-guard at Willingdon Beach then, and the Powell River Company was his boss. In those days Powell River was a real company town trying to attract families to the area by providing such amenities as beaches and life-guards.

Life-guarding was the perfect job for Lockie. The children loved and respected him, and Lockie loved the outdoor life. He later became a draftsman for the company, but his first love was mountain-climbing.

In his younger years P.R. had a hard time finding the right companions to do extensive hiking with. Most of the more interested men were doing shift work and ends seldom happened to meet, but there was a bit more interest in mountain climbing in his later years. As he got older he taught and encouraged a lot of younger men in this sport. "It was like he was trying to pass the information on," Graeme McCahon comments. Some of his earlier companions were R.H. Simmons, Tom Urquart, Ozzie Stevenson, Albert Adams, Don Stewart and Jim Cochrane. These men all climbed to the summit of the 6,200 foot peak called Bear Tooth.

In the late fifties, a young German climber, Christian Schiel, became one of Lockie's friends. Chris was a member of the Munich Alpine Club and climbed to the top of Bear Tooth in July, 1957. He made this trip with Jim Sinclair and George Whyte. This was the fifth time that the climb was completed, and Lockie had been on the other four climbs.

Chris was a different kind of climber from Lockie. Lockie climbed for the beauty and companionship, but Chris climbed to get to the top as quickly as possible. When Chris went to the snow survey cabin it was always important to him that he got there in less time than he did previously. He climbed Bear Tooth several times with various routes on the east face to see if it could be climbed from that side. Challenge, speed and endurance were of great importance to him.

Of course Chris was a European and the circumstances for mountaineering are quite different in Europe. Over there if you want to climb a mountain, you can normally drive right to the base of it, whereas climbing a mountain around Powell Lake, you usually have to count on a day of

Lockie's Table

hacking your way through Devil's Club and Salal before the serious climbing starts. This discourages a lot of climbers, and also discourages one from carrying extra equipment such as pitons, ropes and hammers which are necessary in technical and competitive climbing. "The competi-tiveness of reaching the top in a certain time or by the most difficult route is rather impractical since so much of your time is spent at lower levels fighting the bush," Graeme explains.

Chris climbed "Lockie's Table" with Lockie in 1958. Lockie was 58 years old at the time. Since he was born in 1900 his age was always easy to calculate. In a letter to Graeme, Chris describes the trip this way:

"We climbed up a sort of chimney and arrived at a vertical rock face of about fifteen feet in height which is the key to the climb. This face is broken by a narrow crack through which one must pull oneself up. I had taken a little hatchet along . . . and chopped a wooden peg out of a nearby stump and drove it into the crack. In this way the missing step was provided and all of us, including Lockie, surmounted the face without difficulty. We soon stood happily on the summit. We found a bottle in the cairn and extracted notes from earlier climbers. Among these notes was one note that read, "We two arrived at the peak. Lockie not able to make it. Too old." I think it was a special satisfaction to P.R. to prove them as liars with this climb."

Graeme McCahon's first climbing experience in this area was with P.R. Lockie and Sid Riley in 1963. Sid and Graeme decided to go up Bear Tooth and asked Lockie to escort them. The weather that day was "marginal" but Lockie, knowing how anxious they were to make the trip, went along with the plan. Lockie found the hike strenuous and about half way up the mountain decided to unload his camera gear. He had a heavy movie camera as well as a 120 slide camera, not compact equipment like they have now. With the lightened load, Lockie was able to carry on.

The trail hadn't been used for many years and was fairly overgrown, but Lockie remembered the way. The trail goes up a very steep canyon that is a cleft in the rocks veering up at a forty-five degree angle. At the top of the cleft there is a narrow ledge large enough for a person to squeeze through. On the other side you come to an Alpine plateau covered with heather. This is where the three men set up camp for the night. By this time it was so cloudy they could hardly see Bear Tooth even though they were fairly close to it.

They lit a fire, made supper and crawled into a tent for the night. By the next morning the clouds had lifted enough so they could just see the outline of the mountain.

When you're looking at Bear Tooth from the lake you're really looking at two mountains, Little Bear Tooth is in front of Big Bear Tooth. To climb Big Bear Tooth you have to go around the smaller mountain into the saddle between the two mountains. When they reached the saddle part, P.R. looked at the two younger men and said, "Well, that's as far as I'm going. You're on your own."

Sid and Graeme began "following their noses" through the clouds and up the peak. "It was a good lesson in mountain climbing," Graeme comments. "One of the secrets in climbing is not to worry too much about what's above and what's below; you concentrate on the next rock and decide what you're going to do about that. And under these conditions with clouds all around, all we could see was the next rock."

The two men kept climbing until there was nowhere else to go.

"The top of Bear Tooth is about ten feet square and if you jumped off you'd go hundreds of feet before you hit the bottom," describes Tony Mathews, another local climber. "We couldn't see anything, so reaching the top was kind of an anti-climax," says Graeme. The next year, 1964, the two younger men climbed the mountain again, and this time they were able to see the unbelievable scenery that stretches for miles. "It was also a lot scarier," Graeme chuckles. The men who climbed with Lockie heard many stories, because Lockie was a story-teller, not in the office but in the mountains. "I used to say the higher he climbed the more he talked," Graeme says. "I remember many nights in the snow-survey cabin when my eyes were just dropping out of my head I was so tired, and Old Lockie would talk on and on and tell story after story, and I could not keep my eyes open." Roger Taylor recalls a discussion about the pros and cons of Catholicism that lasted all night.

Graeme remembers the compass story. Lockie was asked to go to the head of the lake to help look for a man who had disappeared. The flumes that the Japanese used for shingle-bolting, were deserted when the Japanese were interned in 1942, but these flumes were handy for hunters because they could walk along them. Apparently this hunter had been back in the mountains, had shot himself a deer, and when he was walking back along the flume with a deer across his shoulders, he fell. With the weight of the deer across his shoulders he broke his neck and died. They found his body lying in the trough of the flume. The search party brought the body out and set off down the lake.

When they reached the lake a heavy fog had set in, but since everyone in the party was familiar with the lake, it didn't cause a lot of concern. The boat was quite slow because at that time there were no high-speed planing hulls only displacement hulls. They had been going down Powell Lake in the fog for several hours, glimpsing only the odd tree on the shore, and a headland here and there, and they decided to check the compass. They discovered they were going west, and since the lake runs north and south, they knew they had turned themselves around some-how. One end of the compass needle was coloured and the other end was plain, and the crew disagreed about which end was pointing north. Finally they agreed, only to discover several hours later that they were at the head of the lake again. They had come down the lake and travelled around Goat Island and back up. Apparently after that Lockie and his friends never forgot which end of the compasss was north.

It was March 1976 that Lockie died, not on the mountain, but at home in bed. He died of a heart attack. His friends agreed that a sudden death such as his was in some ways a blessing. P.R. would have not enjoyed a life where he would have to remain inactive.

A funeral service was held and with a Salvation Army officer present, Lockie's friends participated in conducting a very moving service. Instead of flowers, they placed Lockie's back pack, ice axe and climbing rope on the coffin.

Later on in the summer his friends picked a fine day to go up and scatter Lockie's ashes over the summit of the mountain which was named in his honour.

# The Snow Survey

The following words are taken almost directly from an interview with Graeme McCahon.

I came to Powell River in 1959. At that time a snow survey was regarded as a very tiring job and nobody wanted to do it, but when I came here I thought it sounded wonderful going into the mountains on snow shoes. It sounded adventurous and beautiful, so when I volunteered they couldn't sign me up fast enough. Of course I was born in Australia and snow was completely alien to us. I had never seen snow until I came to Canada. The idea of going off into the mountains in mid-winter, measuring the snow and calculating run-off into the lake sounded absolutely intriguing to me, like a trip across the Sahara Desert would be to someone from here.

The first snow survey was done by P.R. Lockie in 1938. I have pictures of the snow survey cabin being built, and another picture of the cabin just completed, and Old Lockie standing in front of it. It was a very solidly constructed cabin built out of yellow cedar, and I'm sure it still looks the same today as the day it was built. Indestructible. The logs on the cabin floor must be thirty inches in diameter. The floor is made from three or four logs split in half that constitute the whole floor.

In those days the snow survey was a much more involved thing than it is now. They were just starting to collect data on snowfall, trying to correlate that to run-off into the lake, and they didn't have much information to go by so they used to measure the snow in many places, more than they do now.

Graeme McCahon

Building the floor of the snow survey cabin

Gradually they discovered the most reliable data came from the two snow courses that we still measure to this day. One by one the other snow courses were dropped. But in those days the snow survey was a big job and P.R. Lockie used to spend about four weeks out on the trail over the course of the winter. There was a snow survey course up past the junction of Powell and Daniels' Rivers, a place called Silver Creek and another course up near Freda Lake. I think they measured the snowfall up in the Jim Brown Creek area as well.

However, they eventually discovered that one set of measurements taken at the end of the snowfall season, late March, on the two snow courses we use to this day, was adequate. We take sixteen samples on one course and fourteen on the other, and average the readings on each, giving two average readings. It takes a day to do this.

Snow survey cabin

I first did the snow survey in 1960, and I've done it almost every year since then. When I first started to do the snow survey we had to do it on foot. We took a boat to the head of Powell Lake and we carried all our equipment, like snowshoes and food. We hiked to the top snow survey cabin at an elevation of about 3,000 feet. In the summer when there was no snow we could hike it in about three and a half hours, but in the winter it took up to five hours, depending on the snow.

When we got to the cabin the first job was to dig the snow off the roof so we could expose the chimney and light a fire to warm the place up. The next morning we'd put the snowshoes on again and climb to where the snow course was and take fourteen readings. If we were going to measure the second course we'd have to stay over night again. We couldn't do both courses and return to the lake in one day; if we were going to measure both we'd stay the second night, and the third day we'd go back to the lake.

In 1968 they started to do the snow survey by helicopter. Before that, helicopters were too expensive, but by 1968 there was a helicopter stationed over at Campbell River, which was relatively close; it didn't cost too much to bring the helicopter over. And of course, salaries being higher, it paid to rent a helicopter to take people to the snow course and back in one day and not have them away from their mill job for several days.

In November of 1967, Lockie and I went up to the head of the lake and into the cabin. We cleared the few small trees from the swamp just below the cabin. Of course in the winter-time the swamp froze over and was covered with snow and this made a fairly good landing area.

In March of 1968 we went in by helicopter for the first time to try to find this spot but we didn't realize the importance of good weather, and we went on a "marginal" day. We went flying around the mountains in the clouds and weren't able to find the landing area. There was a Mahood logging camp operating at the head of the lake then, and we landed there, went into the cook house and had a cup of coffee, and while we were there the clouds rose a little. The second time around we were able to find the clearing. After we completed the survey on the first course, we moved in the helicopter up to the second course.

The second snow course is different from the first one. It's like a rocky ledge on the side of a mountain. It would be a quarter mile long and about twenty yards wide and it clings rather precariously to the mountain side. We had to find that area from the air too, which is pretty difficult. It is a difficult place to land the helicopter too, because there are tall trees on both sides of the ledge.

The next time we went back we took a chain saw and dropped some trees, and that made it easier to get in by helicopter. From then on it's become easier year by year. We now know we need an exceptionally good day, with at least four thousand feet of visibility, and we won't go unless the weather is right. We've been so many times we know exactly what to look for and we have no difficulty locating both areas.

# Jack Wilson

Jack Wilson left his rural home in Ireland in 1905 and came to New York. He stayed there six years before he moved to Powell River in 1911. At that time the mill was just starting and Powell River was still a frontier town. It was the year that the dam across Powell River broke and the foundations for Number One Paper Machine were washed away. There were only eleven carpenters kept on, and Jack was one of them. At that time it was a toss-up if the mill was going to be re-built. In February the directors of the company decided to continue building.

In 1913 Jack was one of the builders of St. John's Church. Jack used to tell stories about how the workers brought along their mickeys of whiskey. Disposal of the empties, they called them dead men, was no problem. Workers let their empty bottles slide between the "V" joint interior and the outside walls of the building. When the church was finally built there was an impressive ceremony. Jack and a fellow carpenter had built the belfry for the bell that Doctor Henderson donated. Jack had a few anxious minutes when the doctor and a group of other officials climbed up the scaffolding to ring the four hundred pound bell. They weren't sure the scaffolding could hold all that weight.

In 1914 Jack started transporting people up the lake to Tom Ogburn's lodge. The boat he operated was the "Erin Go Brau," and the Powell River Company hired him to do the job. In 1936 the company leased the Rainbow Lodge from Art Lyons and they have used this site for entertaining friends of the company ever since. "More paper was sold at the lodge than in any other place in Canada," Jack used to say. And no wonder. The free refreshments, the superb hunting and fishing and the spectacular scenery provided a most conducive atmosphere for high finance.

Mr. Jack Wilson

Rainbow Lodge

In 1946 there was an earthquake in the area and Jack Wilson was able to make a report to the newspaper of June 26. "We thought we were going to be swept into the lake any moment," he said. "We were sitting down to breakfast when it started, and the first thing we felt was the table shaking. Then we heard a rumble. By that time we knew it was a quake and all of us rushed out. I looked across the water and it certainly was a wonderful sight. The whole of Goat Island was quivering. Boulders the size of a house came crashing down the mountainside and many slides were visible. Suddenly the water in the lake dipped a good foot and we thought the whole dam had gone, but the water came back up and for an hour afterwards, at forty-two second intervals, the water rose and fell. There was no tidal wave, it just went straight up and down."

The summer of 1946, a fire broke out in the boat shed and the "Erin Go Brau" was burned. Three other boats and five rowboats were destroyed as well. Joe Foley built him another boat which they named "Play A Day." Jack was the skipper of this boat until 1958. Two of his most famous guests were Nelson Spencer and Lady Eaton. Apparently Lady Eaton asked Jack when it was the best time to fly fish because she hated worms. Luckily she caught a whopper cut-throat on her first cast and ended up with twelve fish that day.

When he retired in 1958 Jack had many happy memories of times with company guests. He remembered happy sing-songs around campfires and long mellow evenings of swapping yarns. He lived to be over eighty years old.

# Billy-Goat Smith

In 1967, Canada's centennial year, Jack McQuarrie of the Powell River News wrote, "Of all the characters of Powell Lake, Billy-Goat Smith was king."

This statement is true partly because of the rumours that connected Billy-Goat with a famous murder in the States.

The murder happened in 1906 in New York. Society belles and their flashy escorts were dining at a fashionable roof-top supper club in Madison Square Gardens. One of the most impressive couples there was millionaire Harry K. Thaw and his beautiful wife Evelyn Nesbit. Diamonds and wine glasses shimmered in the candlelight while soft music played in the background. Suddenly a shot was heard and Stanford White, a prominent architect was shot. The follow-up trial lasted for eleven weeks. The millionaire Harry K. Thaw was the prime suspect and was convicted of murder in 1907. In a second trial in 1908 Thaw was acquitted on the grounds of insanity because he admitted he had killed White out of jealousy. He claimed his young wife had confessed to intimacies with White before their marriage, but during the first trial he adamantly refused any responsibility in the murder.

A local Powell River man, Evan Sadler, was a newspaper boy at that time and remembers the story being run day after day. It was one of the most publicized murders in history.

Was it coincidence that Mr. Robert Smith came to the West Coast during that era? There is some question regarding the date of his arrival. Some people claim he came as early as 1906, but according to Mr. Ambrose McKinnon he came here in 1910 and started working on construction for Pat Burns and Company. He said it didn't take people long to realize Mr. Smith's hunting ability and soon he was hired to hunt deer to provide the crew with fresh meat. "He was one of the best shots ever on this coast," said Ambrose McKinnon. "I was good myself but used to bring down a deer at thirty yards . . . but he was one of the best with that 30-30 Winchester of his." Mr. McKinnon also reported that in his early days Mr. Smith would occasionally escort hunting parties for the Powell River Company. Once after a long unsuccessful day one of the hunters noticed a herd of goats half a mile away. "I'm going to knock that Billy down," Smith said and he did. The party was amazed to see that goat drop with a bullet through his throat.

"I'm not saying those stories aren't true, I just didn't hear them," Mr. Evan Sadler told me. "I think he came here around 1912 or '13, and he came from Massachusets. He used to get letters from there. I also think he went to live on the lake as soon as he got here."

Evan Sadler was one of the first people to get to know Smith. At that time Evan spent a lot of time working at the Powell Lake boat-houses. This was in the 1920s, the only time that Smith came to down to town regularly. Robert would often be waiting for Evan at the ramp, and he'd usually have a few bottles of beer or saki. "He liked his drink in those days," Evan says.

Mr. Ambrose McKinnon remembers Smith telling this story about his time in the navy before he came to Canada. It seems one day Mr. Smith was passing a small tobacco shop in Liverpool. A woman with a small baby came up to him and asked, "Yankee sailor, will you hold my baby while I get some 'baccy?"

Smith waited until he realized the woman was never going to return for the baby. Finally he stopped a first mate from another ship and asked him to please hold the baby while he went for tobacco. He pulled the same trick the woman did; he went into the shop and out the back door.

"I don't recall him telling that story," Evan says. "But of course it could be true."

Evan Sadler

Smith's life at the lake was a simple one. He made his own flour, hunted his own meat and raised his own vegetables. He was very organized and tidy, always followed a daily routine. In the early days his garden and orchard were such a piece of artistry that people going up the lake were amazed.

This was still pre-war times. At the time there was a boat-house fad going on and anyone who could afford it had a boat and a boat-house on the lake. Some of the permanent residents up the lake resented the intrusion. One cabin that was moored at the head of the lake completely disappeared. Another cabin located at Bear-Tooth Falls was sabotaged. When the owners noticed a strange taste to the sugar they had it analyzed. The strange flavour was from arsenic. About that time a few boats houses were burned down. Because Smith was "different" and rumours were spreading that he was a third party in the New York murder he was a prime suspect, but none of these suspicions was ever confirmed.

Robert Smith enlisted in the army in 1914 and was away from his homestead until 1918. He was put in the machine gun section at the Vernon Army camp. When the other Powell River men tried to associate with him, he ignored them. After they returned home Jack Wilson asked Smith what was going on. "Why wasn't I taken over to France with you fellows?" he asked. "I'm a better shot than any of you."

In 1918 he immediately returned to his own world at the head of the lake. While he was away, in 1917 the first car had arrived in Powell River. By 1929 there were only three in the district, but right after that the car population mushroomed and Powell Lake, which had been the weekend home of the town people became almost deserted as boat owners were among the first to own cars. Many boats lay unused in their houses on the river.

It was during the 1920s that Mr. Smith became interested in education. Nick Hudemka, another hermit on the lake, always claimed that Smith was an Adirondack "hill-billy" to begin with. Ambrose McKinnon remembers going up to Smith's place and Smith would try out fancy words on him. "What are you trying to prove?" Ambrose asked, and Smith admitted he was studying the Webster dictionary, and didn't have too many opportunities to try out his new vocabulary. "He always was an ardent reader," Evan explains. "He would always order books through the mail, and his friends all brought him books too." Later in his life people who met Smith always assumed he was a well-educated man. He was, even though he was self-educated.

The Powell River Company raised the lake again in 1924. The water flooded over Mr. Smith's beautiful orchards and gardens. The company let him know that he would be compensated for his losses with a cheque for $6,600 but to get the money he would have to present his land deeds to the company. Smith wanted the money but didn't trust his deeds to the mail or to any other person. Furthermore he wasn't fussy about leaving his place at the lake. Finally the company decided to summons him.

This was a problem. Even at the best of times Smith's place was not the most welcoming. Once when Smith was away prospecting, some people from town raided his apple orchards, and ever since then he had a sign posted at the entrance of his harbour that read: "No dogs or Powell River residents allowed." And of course everyone was aware of the murder-rumours and the fact that he always kept his rifle ready to scare off unknown characters.

Jack Wilson, the company lake guide was the lucky person selected for the duty. Jack was sworn in as sheriff to serve the summons. "I took the summons up to him, and I also kept my gun close at hand. He took the summons, looked at me for a few minutes, then hoisted his rifle to his shoulder. I thought for sure I'd had it . . . however, he seemed to be thinking it over, then he shrugged and walked toward his cabin. I was sweating blood, I can tell you."

Luckily, Smith did not hold a grudge against Jack. A few weeks later Smith went up to Jack in town and offered to buy him a drink. He had been to Vancouver with the company manager and "had been barbered and had bought some clothes. He really was a fine-looking man."

Although Smith resented the flooding of his property it worked out for him in the long run. He was able to buy a boat, and after that he always had a little cash hidden away.

Smith was never one to part with his money very easily. The people at Olsen Landing found him to be quite a borrower. In an interview with Golden Stanley, Harry Gothard recalled how he would always be borrowing tea or sugar or something like that. Of course groceries were always a problem because he depended on outside people to bring him his supplies, people like George Sing, one of the brothers who owned a grocery store at the shingle mill at the town end of Powell Lake, and Nick Hudemka, the hand-logger who went up and down the lake more frequently than he did. Often the people who delivered groceries for him would stop doing it because of squabbles over the price.

One old-timer who used to deliver Smith's supplies and do him all sorts of favours got a shock in the summer of 1929 when a police officer came to his bunkhouse in Riverside and presented him with a warrant for his arrest. Robert Smith had charged him with stealing a timer off his motor.

Apparently the fellow had borrowed the timer and hadn't been able to return it because he had been working three weeks steady at the paper mill.

The old-timer told the police the story and then the policeman recalled that a bottle with a note in it had been found at the end of the lake.

The note said: Smith not well. Bring help.

The two men went up the lake to sort things out. Both were nervous not knowing what kind of reception they would get. Smith came running down to meet them and when he saw the constable he looked at his friend and said, "Christ, you didn't have to bring a cop with you."

I don't know what the friend said, but it was probably something like: "What the hell do you think you're doing reporting me for stealing... you know I borrowed the timer. I didn't steal it. I can't believe you doing that after all the favours I've done for you. What kind of a friend are you anyway?"

Smith was suitably remorseful. "I've been sick and I was out of my mind when I wrote that." The policeman ordered Smith to come down to the hospital. There Dr. Marlatt discovered that the hermit had a heart condition. His friend visited him in the hospital and they never had any disagreements after that.

Around 1931, Smith got some goats from Tom Lambert in Paradise Valley. This sounds like a simple procedure but he transported the goats by row boat. Goats reproduce like rabbits and it wasn't long before he had about twenty. You could smell those goats for miles around. He became very fond of the creatures and was sometimes jealous when they took a liking to visitors. He had a humorous way of talking to the goats about his visitors when he wanted to say something uncomplimentary. Of course it didn't take people in the area long to label the hermit as "Billy-Goat Smith."

It was around 1934 that Billy-Goat decided to quit drinking. Up to that time he would always order a bottle up with is groceries, but now he said, he saw the light. Maybe it was his concern about his poor heart that drove him to this decision, or maybe it was his new association with some Jehovah Witnesses from town. Billy-Goat's philosophy of life matched the Witness doctrine in some ways. Since his short time out in the world had been during World War One, he must have had a negative impression of the human race; he hated war and was disillusioned with mankind. He often commented to visitors that "It must be tough out there."

It also appears that Billy-Goat believed the second coming to be close at hand. There was one bright star in the sky he would watch for hours. He believed it to be a modern equivalent of the star of Bethlehem.

After Smith's decision to stop drinking he became more of a recluse than ever. One social event that surprised Jack Wilson happened in 1935. That winter Jack was escorting a group of people up the lake on a company survey. They stopped at Smith's Landing. When Smith realized there were women in the boat he pushed the boat away and yelled at Jack:

"Wilson, you ought to know better than to bring women around here, and me with my knees out of my pants, and not shaved or dressed."

Later that evening the party staying at Feckner's Lodge, near Smith's place, were surprised when an unannounced gentleman visitor, Mr. Robert Smith, all shaved and dressed in a pressed blue suit, arrived to spend a pleasant evening conversing with his former nurse, Caroline Smith.

This was one of the few times that his friends saw him have anything to do with a woman, although he was usually cordial to the wives of the men he knew.

In 1937 Billy-Goat 's boat was wrecked in a storm, and from that time on he seldom came to town. Once in October of 1949 he came to see the play "Thark," and that trip was so unusual it made the news.

Groceries became more of a problem with no boat, and he became more dependent on others for supplies. He ordered staples from Spencers in Vancouver about twice a year. Bill Merrit of Lund remembers meeting the hermit during the 1950s when he came to the logging camp to borrow some tea. Bill wasn't very impressed with the hermit. "Get out of here," he said. At that time Bill was working at a logging camp up past Manson Landing.

In 1959 Smith's relatives from Oregon came to visit him and tried to persuade him to return to civilization. His nephew, Marion Smith reported that "His arthritis was so bad that in order to put on his coat, he would put one arm in a sleeve and then use a stick to pull the other sleeve around so he could put his arm into it."

It was early in 1960 that Bertram Wilson, the game warden, and Sgt. Rothwell, a pilot of the RCMP aircraft became concerned about the old man's welfare. "I realized how isolated he had been when I mentioned a car one day," Bertram recalls. "Billy-Goat said that he had ridden in one once."

It was spring of 1960 that Mr. Bertram Wilson made a trip by plane with a mail-order supply including a rubber-tired wheel-barrow. Bertram remarked that this would be the first modern piece of equipment ever to reach Smith's property. However, on arriving at Smith's place they could see that he was failing. They suggested that he return to town with them to get some medical attention, but he refused and in his independent way replied, "If a doctor was up this way he could drop in."

This bothered Mr. Wilson for a long time because two weeks later some Jehovah Witnesses found him dead; he had fallen forward into the shiny red wheel-barrow.

Mr. Bertram Wilson and Sgt. Rothwell went up in the plane to

Billy-Goat Smith and his nephew

collect the body. During that same year, 1960, Sgt. Rothwell and his crew were killed in a plane crash.

I guess Billy-Goat could have predicted the way the despised residents of Powell River reacted to the news of his death. Some residents from town went up and ransacked the place taking whatever they could find. They even took the goats.

Jack Wilson was the one who found the money. About $1,000 in old bills, some American and a few of the old large Canadian one-dollar bills. Jack remembered that one day he had delivered some goat fodder to the cabin. When Jack asked Billy-Goat for payment he went away for a few minutes. When he came back, Jack could smell a peculiar odor to the money, and asked what it was. "What do you think it smells like?" Billy-Goat asked.

"Goats," Jack teased. "Everything around here smells like goats."

"You're wrong," he said. "It's dirt."

That's how Jack knew where the money was buried.

It appears that the exact truth about Smith and his connection to the New York murder, died with him. We have no historical proof that he was in any way involved with the Stanford White murder. Robert Bonner Smith was never wanted officially.

Art Lyons, a Powell River man who died in the sixties, said in a taped interview that Billy-Goat did the shooting and that Thaw was blamed for it. Lyons also said that while the Thaws were leaving the night club, Mrs. Thaw got the gun from Smith and slipped it into her husband's top coat. That way she would get rid of her husband and her ex-lover. Mrs. Thaw never paid Smith and for that reason Smith never trusted a woman.

A *Collier's* magazine article implicated a third party as a gunman in the murder. According to the *West Coast* a hit-man in the murder escaped by train. This article was used as a basis for the movie: *The Girl in the Red Velvet Swing*.

Jack Wilson remarked to Jack McQuarrie that Smith told him once that if by some unforseen circumstances he should visit his family in the States he would never take a train. Is this merely coincidence, or is it more evidence to substantiate the theory that he was a hit-man in the murder?

"He was a man you could never get behind. He was nervous," remembers Stewart Lambert. Billy-Goat stayed in their house once when Stewart was a child.

The strongest evidence that Billy-Goat was involved in the murder is the word of people who knew him . . . at the same time there is always one haunting fear: it would take just one imaginative story-teller to link Billy-Goat with the New York murder.

My personal theory is that Billy-Goat was involved in a murder in the States, but not in the Stanford White murder. I think it involved a woman, his girlfriend or lover, I am only guessing, and hope that one day we will find out what really happened.

# Powell Lake
## Today

Powell Lake is still one of the most beautiful and least known areas of the province. There is still a lot of wild-life around its shores. There's black bear, deer, grouse, wolves and mountain goats. After the thirties there was very little activity on the lake until the early seventies, but gradually people began to build house-boats and take them up the lake again. Now there are more house-boats on the lake than ever.

Gerhard Tollas, a Powell River map-maker and canoe enthusiast, used to wish that people around Powell River and the tourists visiting the area would take the time to appreciate the spectacular wilderness scenery available. It was with this in mind that in 1976 he conceived the idea of the possibilities of a canoe route which could be used by the public. The idea was exciting. Not only could the route boost tourism in the area, it would also provide people with the opportunity to get in touch with nature and give the lakes the respect and appreciation that the wilderness environment deserves.

It wasn't until September of 1982 that residents of Powell River were able to begin work on the canoe route which links eight lakes; included in the route are Goat, Windsor, Dodd, Ireland, Nanton, Horseshoe, Lois and Powell Lake. The project was unique in that it involved the co-operation and collaboration of the B.C. Forest Service Recreation Program and the Powell River Chamber of Commerce, and the joint Federal Provincial Employment Bridging Assistance Program.

One of the workers biggest surprises was finding a Japanese road at an old shingle bolt camp. The Japanese built the road from cedar slabs in the 1930's. Barry Auger, project superintendent, told the Vancouver Sun that the Japanese "had 15 teams of horses in the bush and used sleds with greased wooden runners on the road." Back in the camp they found boom chains, conveyor belts and quarter-inch wire all over the place.

The canoe route is well-planned with canoe rests built of logs about every three hundred metres along the portages. Campsites, wharves and cedar picnic tables are conveniently placed along the trails. There are almost eighty bridges ranging from one just ten feet long, to a trestle bridge 127 feet long. "One bridge is built out of a single log 86 feet long," Bob Rebantad reports. Along the trail historical signs mark points of interest.

For anyone who wants to canoe on Powell Lake, the lake is safest in the early morning or evening. Every day from noon until about 7 p.m. the mountains tend to siphon up warm air from the ocean and this creates quite a strong wind.

With the official opening of the canoe-trail in May of 1983, a new chapter in the life of Powell Lake began. At last it is time for this beautiful and mysterious lake to be used, not abused. At last it is time for this lake to be recognized and acknowledged.

# References

## Footnotes

1 Community Portraits: George F. Smarge, The Powell River News, Feb. 12, 1959, p. 9.
2 Barry Rice, Olsen Valley: A local community that thrived and then died, The Powell River Progress, Feb. 23, 1977, p. 9.
3 Award Contract to Divert River, The Powell River News, Aug. 10, 1955, p. 1.
4 Mark Vonnegut, The Eden Express, Praeger Publishers, 1976, p. 50.
5 Ibid. p. 50.
6 Ibid., p. 91.

## Sources

### 1. Books

McArthur, Craig J. BC CENTENNIAL OF LOGGING. Vancouver, A Gordon Black publication, 1966.

Trower, Peter. BETWEEN THE SKY & THE SPLINTERS. Madeira Park, Harbour Publishing, 1974.

Vonnegut, Mark. THE EDEN EXPRESS. A Bantam book published with arrangement with Frank E. Taylor, Praeger Publishers, 1976.

White, Howard. THE RAINCOAST CHRONICLES. Madeira Park, Raincoast Historical Society, 1972-1976.

### 2. Newspapers

THE POWELL RIVER NEWS. 1928-83. Powell River Museum.

THE POWELL RIVER PROGRESS. 1977. Powell River Museum.

THE VANCOUVER SUN. June 1983.

# Index

Adams, Albert, 72
Aleutian Islands, 61
Allman, Harold, 64
Anderson, Andy, 32, 67-70
Anderson, Clara (nee
  Olson), 32, 67-71
Arena, 65
Auger, Barry, 91
Baumons, 33
Bears, 28, 43, 46-47, 52, 67
Bear Tooth Mountain, 54,
  60, 71-72, 74
Boats, "Erin Go Brau," 80
  "Toklat," 51, 56-57
  "The Toothpick," 27,
  32-33
  "The Tropic Sea," 51
  "Vernu," 57
Borer, 33-34, 57
Bridges, 14, 17, 49, 70, 91
Brooks-Bidlake, 17, 31, 49
Brooks, Dr. Dwight, 18
Burg and Johnson, 56
Cabins, 20, 47-49, 85
Cameron, George, 54
Canoe Route, 91
Carter Brothers, 69
Cassiar Island, 16-17, 20,
  23, 56
Cedar Street, 17, 37
Chanson, Gus, 29-30, 34
Chinese, 31, 35, 50-51,
  54, 57
Chippewa Baby, 50
Cochrane, Jim, 72
Cockrill, Gladys, 52
Collins, D.R., 66
Company store, 37, 57-58
Conservation issues,
  16-17, 34-36
Conversion Dam, 34
Cook, Manford, 66
Daniels River, 47
Diotte Airways Ltd., 67
Diotte Cessna 140, 66
Diotte, William, 66
Dominion Day
  celebrations, 20, 38
Dycks, Gordie, 35
Earthquake, 82
Eaton, Lady, 82
Endo, Mitsuru, 61
Errico, Joe, 37-38
False Bay, 66

Feckner's Lodge, 88
Fifth Avenue
  Dress Shop, 57
Fires, 26, 57, 64-65, 67
Fishing, 17, 35, 41, 80
Foch, 30
Foley, 29
Foley, Joe, 82
Foort, Terry, 49
Foote, Bob, 59
Freda Lake, 78
Galoca, John, 65
Gaston, Bill, 51
Gilbert, August, 30
Giovani Lake, 38
Gishards, 29
Goat Lake, 12, 35, 41-42,
  47, 50, 54, 67, 75, 82, 91
Goats, 28, 70, 83, 90-91
Goffin, R.H., 65
Golf course, 32, 68
Gordon, Emile, 59-60
Gothard, 27, 86
Government wharf, 19,
  49, 51
Harper, Jack, 33
Hart, Don, 48
Haslam Lake, 14
Hastings Mill, 69
Haywire Bay, 68
Head of lake, 13, 50, 85
Healing gathering, 40
Heating, in townsite, 15-16
  in Shingle Mill
  Community, 54
Henderson, Dr., 20, 80
Heritage Village, 70
Hippies, 34, 39-40
Hudemka, Nick, 44-49, 85
Hukster, 59
Hult, 5
Jameson, 17, 38, 50-57,
  60, 65
Jamieson, William, 34
Japanese, 31-32, 50, 54,
  60-63, 75, 91
Joan Lake, 47
Kendrick, Jimmy, 37
Kinishi, 63
Knimps, 30
Lakeview Lumber
  Company, 68-70
Lambert, Stewart, 90
Lang Bay, 37

Lang, Norman, 20
Lasser, Robert and
  Walter, 32
Laundry, 51, 57-59
Little, Charlie, 54
Lockie, P.R., 71-76
Lockie's Table, 71, 73, 76
Logging, 18, 26, 34, 41,
  44-49, 79
Loukes, 57
Lyons, Art, 38, 80, 90
Mahara, Nehemi, 63
Mahood, 79
Manson Landing, 88
Mantoani, 48
Marlatt, 68, 87
Martin, James, 65
Mathews, Tony, 38, 48
Merrick, 59
Merril and Ring, 34
Merrit, Bill, 88
Michegan and Puget
  Sound Lumber Co., 67
Michegan Landing, 18, 49
Morrison, 57
Mowat Bay, 31, 51, 69-70
Myrtle Point, 41
McCahon, Graeme, 72-73
MacIntyre, "Bat," 60
McKinnon, Ambrose, 83
MacMillan Bloedel Ltd., 35
McMillan Creek, 61
McQuarrie, Jack, 82, 90
McWhirter, D.R., 66
Nakamura, 60-61
Nakatsu, Jim, 63
Nesbit, Evelyn, 82
Norton, 29, 33
O'Brien, George, 65
Ogburn, Tom, 35-36, 80
Okeover, 34
Olsen, 25
Olsen Creek Logging
  Company, 65
Olsen Valley, 25-35
Olson, Ole, 27, 32, 67
Olsons, 25, 52
Palmers, 28
Parks, 30
Pat Burns and Co., 83
Patricia Theatre, 18, 36
Pavid, Henry, 57
Penstocks, 15
Petersons, 29

Petit, Pierre, 29-30, 34
Pilling, Bill, 59
Plisson, Tom, 31, 33
Post office, 23, 30
Powell, Dr. Israel, 14
Powell Lake Monster, 23-24
Powell River Company, 14-19, 23, 33-34, 37, 47, 57-58, 65, 71-72, 80, 85
Powell River Dam, 16-17, 61, 80
Powell River News, 41, 58, 63-65, 69, 82
Pre-emptions, 26, 32, 37-38
Prospecting, 13, 17, 41
Railroad, 18, 36, 49, 67
Rainbow Lodge, 47, 80
Rebantad, Bob, 92
Reserve Army, 61
Restaurants, 51, 57
Riley, Sid, 72
Riverside, 86
Rodmay, 59
Rolandis, 29, 32
Rothwell, 88
Rowleys, 29, 32
RCMP, 48, 52
Sadler, Evan, 23, 38, 83-85
St. John's Church, 80
St. Lukes Hospital, 30
Salmon, 17
Scanlon, 26
Scheibers, 40
Schiel, Christian, 72
Schools, 29-30, 40
Second Narrows, 47, 49

Seixas, Peter, 40
Shingle Mill Community, 50-52, 57, 63-66
Shingles, 17, 31, 49-57, 63-66
Shultz, 29
Silver Creek, 78
Simards, 30-33
Simmons, R.H., 71
Sims, Ray, 65
Sinclair, Jim, 72
Sing, George, 86
Sing Lee, 51, 53, 57
Sing, Sam, 54
Sliammon, 12, 17, 28, 41
Smarge, 37
Smith, Caroline, 88
Smith, Marion, 88
Smith, Robert (Billy Goat), 82-91
Snow survey, 71, 76-77
Sombertons, 57
Soo Jan Kee, 61
Spatari, Sam, 39
Spencer, Nelson, 82
Springer, 18
Stanley, Golden, 23-25, 27, 38, 86
Steele, 57
Stevenson, Ozzie, 72
Stewart, Don, 72
Stillwater, 18, 63
Taylor, Roger, 75
Tesquiot, 12
Texada Island, 35, 43, 60
Thaw, Harry K., 82
Theodosia, 26, 28
Toequenun, 28

Tolfeba, 23
Tollas, Gerhard, 91
Toma, Chief, 24
Topography, 14
Town Crier, 56
Trapping, 67
Unions, 54, 69-70
Union Steamships, 19
Urquart, Tom, 72
Uzell, Bill, 41
Van Bilderbeck, 37-38
Vonnegut, Mar, 39
Wales, Miss, 57
Wasat & Mowat Shingle Mill, 69
Water, 14-15, 40
Westview Wharf, 19, 66
Wheeler, William, 65
White, Stanford, 83
Whitley, 34
Whyte, George, 72
Wilcocks, 51, 53, 56
Wildlife, 42, 45, 70
Williams, Charles, 66
Willingdon, 18, 49, 72
Wilshire and Lant, 57
Wilson, Bertram, 88
Wilson, Jack, 80, 85-87, 89-90
Winegarden, Nelson, 66
Woodward, Curly, 14-21, 23, 38, 60
World War II, 60-61
Yinling, 70
Yip, Tom, 51, 59
York Island, 61

**Photographs by:**
Juliet Potter — pages 13, 15, 25, 26, 84.
Museum Photo — pages 18, 19, 20, 21, 22, 33, 36, 50, 52, 55, 62, 68, 69, 71, 73, 77 (bottom), 78, 81, 89.
Oren Olson — pages 27, 28.
The Simards — page 30.
John Louke — page 39.
Barry Lang — page 45.
Graeme McCahon — page 77 (top).